PLAY IT FOR REAL
Christian ways of doing drama

Roger Grainger

First published by Eastmoor Books
ISBN 0 9528653 3 5

Printed in England by FM Repro Ltd. Tel: (01924) 411011

Dedicated to
The Pamela Keily Players

Roger Grainger is a Parish Minister who is also a Professional Actor.
He is Drama Adviser for the Diocese of Wakefield.

CONTENTS

PROLOGUE

Ann's Play

A small circle of people standing in the corner of the room around a space that's not very wide, but wide enough. They are looking inward to the centre of the space, where a child is playing. She's walking round and round, looking at the floor. Sometimes she kicks at something with her toe, something like an imaginary stone or perhaps a twig. For her, the people standing round aren't there; she isn't aware of being the centre of attention. She scans the floor looking for imaginary things to kick. A cough (somebody in the audience) - she throws a terrified glance towards the corner of the room; everyone freezes, holding their breath as they catch her fear. Then she's back with her game, squatting down in the middle of the circle clutching something to herself, rocking backwards and forwards, humming softly. Some of us can see the twig she's holding, some can't.

CHAPTER I: WHAT IS A PLAY?

Before we start to look at the business of acting plays in church we have to look more closely at what plays really are so that we can be quite sure that church is the right place to do them. 'Do' is the right word to use, because it is what drama actually means. It comes from *drao*, Greek for 'I do'. However drama isn't just doing things, it's doing them in a certain kind of way. The Oxford Dictionary says it means "a set of events having the unity and progress of a play and leading to catastrophe or consummation." 'Catastrophe' and 'consummation' refer to the two main kinds of drama, tragedy and comedy; plays designed to make you cry or laugh - or perhaps laugh until you cry. The dictionary doesn't actually say what a play is, however; instead it refers us back to the definition of drama, so we shall have to find our own way of making sense of what makes plays different from other kinds of doing.

The simplest plays are the ones we act by ourselves. For her play about the child in a concentration camp, Ann only needed one person - herself. One thing about herself was particularly important, and that was her imagination. Without Ann's imagination there wouldn't have been a play at all. The other thing she needed, to make it a play and not simply a game, was an audience - in other words, us, the people watching. These two things meant that Ann could do more than simply play, as you do when you play a game, she could *do a play*. She could present what she was imagining to an audience. We call this performing a play. It's a way of making our imagination more vivid by sharing it with others. Plays always involve other people by latching onto their imaginations to create a special kind of imagined situation, what we call 'the world of play'.

I say that a play isn't a game, and that's true. On the other hand there's something about a play which is very like a game, a kind of shared game. What I mean is plays leave you to join in or not according to how you feel, like games do. They don't latch onto your imagination unless you want them to. Plays need our permission to be plays: we have to agree that what we are doing is in fact a play. This is very important, so let's just think about it for a moment.

In the example of the play described above, Ann was asked to act something out for us. In other words, she was invited to 'do a play' for us. She could have invited somebody to take part in it with her, but she didn't do this; she preferred to act the play by herself and use the rest of us as the audience. So she gathered us together in a circle, leaving as much room in the middle as she thought she would need, and the play began. We knew when it began and when it ended. To begin with we were standing in a circle, waiting for something to happen. Our attention was focused on the space before us, empty except for Ann, who was kneeling on the floor. Suddenly she began to move. She stood up, and the play had begun. When she had finished acting, she squatted down again. We waited for her to move but she didn't: the play was over. It had ended and we all knew it.

Afterwards, when the session was over we told our friends about it: Ann did this marvellous play, you should've been there . . . This, I think was a particularly good example of what a play really is, even though it only had one person in it (and the audience, of course). It's a good example because it was perfectly honest about itself. I am a play, it said. I am make-believe. You must imagine what I'm showing to you, sharing with you, is happening, really happening, or nothing will happen at all. It's no good being half-hearted about this. If you keep saying to yourself, "It's only a play, it's not really true", it won't even be that; it won't even be 'only' a play.

This, then, is the secret about plays: you know *they're going to be* plays and you know *they have been* plays. In between, you don't think about it; you haven't time, you're too busy concentrating on what's going on. At least you should be if you're really taking part, either as an actor or a member of the audience. Whichever you are, the invitation to *share* a play takes up most of your imagination and concentration. Imagination is a very powerful thing. When it is shared it grows out of all proportion. As I said before, imagination creates its own world. So far as plays go, it's all you need. It's a very powerful thing and most of us have got it, thank God.

Imagination and concentration. You hear a lot about the magical quality people call 'talent' - "Oh she's very talented, of course. She always was. I couldn't possibly do anything like that, I haven't the talent." This may be true; but don't forget, what this person is saying is that they can't concentrate and haven't any imagination - well, not enough anyway. Because when it comes to acting in plays that is what talent really is. We can all describe things dramatically, *as if* they were really happening - we do this a lot, in 'ordinary' conversation in the 'ordinary' world. What we have to learn to do if we want to put on plays and act in them is to concentrate as hard as we can on the as-if point, and trust the audience's promise that they will give us as much support as they can by really using their own imagination and concentration to play along with us.

If you let people know in an unmistakable way that what is going to happen next is a play, they may not immediately like the idea very much and may even protest quite loudly, but they will start to co-operate because you're asking them to do something which is so natural, so much a part of human nature, that they actually have to make a positive effort to refuse to join in. On the other hand, we none of us enjoy being tricked into taking part. I remember once going to a performance of a play and when I got there I was told that there had been a change of plans - it was going to be a rehearsal instead. The people on the stage weren't playing parts, they were simply actors getting ready to act. In fact this wasn't true at all: they were characters in the play. It was a play about actors, you see. It was very clever and real, and would have moved me a lot - if I hadn't been so angry at being tricked in this way.

In my opinion, you shouldn't lay traps for the audience like this - and you certainly shouldn't do it in church. My reason for saying this is quite simple: it's because theatre - by which I mean plays of all kinds - depends on honesty. Imagination, concentration - and honesty. The play about actors certainly grabbed my imagination, and I concentrated on what was going on as if it vitally concerned me personally and could change my life. How I wish I had been invited to feel like this instead of being manipulated into it!

A lot of people think that all plays are like that - a way of pulling a fast one on the audience. Speaking personally, I was brought up to distrust what was usually called 'play-acting'. I think a lot of English people are, and not only English people either. I get a distinct impression that this attitude is still very much around, even though we all spend so much time watching and enjoying plays on TV. Perhaps we think that plays and things like that are all right so long as you're a special kind of person. The people who are in TV plays are special in that sense. They're 'professionals' and 'celebrities'; it's fine to read about them in magazines and on chat-shows, but ordinary people aren't like that, and most of us wouldn't really want to be either. We enjoy the difference. In the old days we called it glamour: Hollywood was built up out of it.

The trouble is, it gets in the way when we want to do some ordinary, down-to-earth acting ourselves. Because people can't be star performers they assume they can't act at all. So they never try. We shall be saying more about this later on. For the time being I want to concentrate on another reason why people are suspicious about actors and acting. It isn't only because the thought of going on stage or before the cameras makes us so very nervous ourselves; it's a deeper kind of reason than that. It's something to do with a feeling that people have that acting itself is somehow insincere. We shouldn't pretend that something is happening when it isn't; we shouldn't pretend to be someone else when we are really ourselves. To do these things is to behave in a way that is basically dishonest; and yet drama and theatre consist in this and nothing else. From this point of view, plays are nothing better than elaborate confidence tricks, and honest, straightforward people oughtn't to have anything at all to do with them!

I think that this idea crops up in our minds when we consider the business of acting plays - or sketches or monologues or anything involving drama - in *church*. It has to be taken seriously because everything else to do with drama and theatre depends on its. So is it true, or isn't it? Well, of course it's true. I've already given an example of the way in which a play can trick the audience into believing what it says by the skill with which it pretends not to be a play at all. I, for one, really believed that what I had arrived at was a rehearsal, not a play, and the people on stage were simply getting ready to act and not actually acting at all. It takes skill to kid people like this, of course - but we've all had a lot of practice at kidding people one way or another; and if we haven't done it ourselves (and which of us hasn't?), we've certainly had it done to us.

So it wouldn't be honest to defend plays by saying that they don't involve pretence. Of course they do. We imagine something as if it were so and then pretend it is. We not only pretend it is, but we do our best to make it look and sound, or even smell and feel as if it is. By the time we've finished working on it nobody is in any doubt at all that *something* is happening here. It's this that we call a play. It begins as 'let's pretend'; but now it has a reality of its own. As-if has become a real human event, with real people taking part in it. We discuss it afterwards, delivering our own judgement as to whether it was good or bad, boring or exciting, too long or too short, and each of us knows what the others mean. As we said at the beginning, a play is an experience that people share. There's no pretence in this part - people say exactly what they think! We have given flesh to our imagination and the result is something which we can stand back and look at, or draw closer to and become involved in; the point is, it's something that exists in the real world, not just in the imagination. Certainly, somebody or other made it up: the point is that we are in a position to say whether what they made up has turned out to be true or not.

This, then, is the answer to the question about whether plays are true or not. In one sense they aren't; they involve people pretending to be other people, and show events, places and times that may never have existed - certainly not like that, anyway. But in another sense it can turn out that they are not only true but some of the truest experiences we ever have. It has been said that the truest things about life can't be kept to oneself: they have to be shared. Love is the best example. It's also true that they can't be simply described either. In order to be experienced as true, something has to be *lived*. In other words, it must be discovered by somebody as true about the life they know, as they themselves know it; and then it must be shared. Plays and stories demonstrate invisible truth, the invisible truths that govern human life and death, in context. In stories and plays we see these things at work in the world.

The best way that Jesus could get across some idea of what God's love is like, what it can actually mean to living men and women, was by making up a story about a man with two sons. He took a piece of fiction and used it to embody the greatest and most profound truth that we can possibly know - the truth in which we 'live and move and have our being'. We call this 'having a message'. The function of plays and stories is to convey a message about the meaning and significance of life in a recognisable picture of what life is actually like. Jesus' parables are wonderful examples of this; in fact the word parable means 'throwing together'. A parable is a story in which two things are brought together in order to shed light on each other: in other words, a story with a message. The story may be specially made up, or based on an actual happening. In the same way, of course, the message may be false or true, but if the story framework strikes a chord in the lives of the people it is directed at, then the message will comes across as being true. The important thing to remember is the fact that a fictional story may have a genuine message.

Just as stories come in all sizes, so do messages, which can be other things besides 'true' or 'false'. They can be serious or funny, happy or sad, sentimental or ironic, religious or secular, subtle or obvious. Whatever they are, however, they are always present. A story always tells us something about life one way or another: it always has a message. Plays and stories which try hard not to communicate any kind of message simply end up telling everyone that, so far as they are concerned, such things are futile or meaningless - which is, of course, a powerful message about life. For instance, a play in which nothing very much happens has the effect of communicating the idea that life itself is like that. We aren't forced to believe it, of course; but we may come away feeling it to be a distinct possibility ...

So people who write, produce and act in plays have a real responsibility towards the audience. Even the simplest play can be very powerful. If you believe in what the play has to say then the combination of its truths and your sincerity will certainly get across even if you don't think you're very good at the business of putting plays on and acting in them. I don't think you should let this worry you, though; it's one reason why you shouldn't let lack of skill and experience get in your way. Sincerity and belief in your message - the play's message - will go far towards seeing you through. Above all, as I said, concentrate on doing it and it will speak for itself. If games are there for us to lose ourselves in, the same kind of thing goes for plays. They are there to help us forget our self consciousness by pretending to be someone else: we can let 'someone else' deliver the message! This is what we mean when we talk about actors wearing masks "not to conceal but to reveal themselves". We shall be coming back to this in the next chapter, which is mainly about acting.

The main point about this chapter, however, concerns the play itself. Although plays imitate things that happen in life, they are real happenings in themselves. Because they are a special way of getting things across clearly and vividly, they can be very useful ways of teaching - but that isn't all there is to say about them. There's more to it than that, much more. Plays are living experiences not just visual aids. On their own accord they say something vital about themselves, something which doesn't only depend on what the director, the actors or even the author may want them to say. A play says something vital about being alive, being human. It demonstrates human relationships, human situations, human experiences not simply by talking about these things but by *being* them. Because it is a play rather than a letter or an essay, a story or a sermon, it will already be saying something that can't be said in any other way. Plays reveal rather than deliver - it's as Jesus says about his parables: "He (or she) who has ears to hear ..." What we see is not simply an imitation of life, but a living example of life itself, something we can join in and live through. We aren't simply told something: we can join in and discover our own version of it. We share imaginations.

This is a very important thing to remember - that plays don't tell you something straight out; they encourage you to find out for yourself. This is why plays are so useful for sharing the Christian faith. They leave people free to make up their own minds and 'look before they leap'. You don't have to accept what a play seems to be saying. People who write plays - particularly plays for church - would often like you to accept what they want to say without argument. Unfortunately (from their point of view), plays don't work like that. If you try and force people to accept your point of view in a play you run the risk of defeating your object. Characters in a play have many different things to say: the fact that they don't always agree is what a play is about. Audiences have to be left free to choose the one they want to agree with. It won't always be the one who argues most persuasively - or even perhaps the one the author of the play intended. Hamlet said about the Player Queen: "The lady doth protest too much, methinks."

Plays come in all shapes and sizes. They are often divided into short sections called 'scenes' and longer ones called 'acts' which are groups of scenes gathered together. The scenes in an act hang together and are often different aspects of the same situation, so you could say that the play's story moves along act by act rather than scene by scene - unless, of course, you don't bother with acts and simply have a succession of scenes, each one moving the story forward. This makes no difference, as long as they *do* move it forward, so that people who see the play are aware that it has a kind of basic shape, starting somewhere and ending somewhere else. A play needs to have a beginning, a middle and an end. This is something to do with the way that plays are put together. It isn't obvious to you when you're actually watching them and getting involved in them, but if you think about it afterwards you'll realise this is true. If it weren't you'd still be sitting there waiting for something to happen. Even plays which are about nothing happening have a beginning, a middle and an end. They have a section leading into an idea, in which nothing really happens; a section in which you become conscious of the lack of action by becoming involved in it; and a section when you realise what it is you've seen - a play about nothing happening and what it's like when it doesn't! And it has taken three distinct sections - acts, scenes, or parts of the same single scene if it's a one-scene play - to get the idea firmly across to you.

If you can do this with a play in which nothing happens (I mean get something across as well as this), imagine what you can do with plays in which things do happen and are seen and felt to happen - which, of course, is most plays, certainly the ones you will want to do in church (and the ones people will want to watch!). Similarly, the plays you make up for yourself will need to centre upon something you think is important and want to get across in as unforgettable a way as you can. These too will have to have the right kind of beginning, middle and end. Teachers have a saying about the way to get something across to a class: "Tell 'em you're going to do it, do it, and tell 'em you've done it." This is very, very true about plays. I don't mean you should always announce that a play is going to be performed and afterwards, before the audience starts to leave, jump in and thank everybody for coming and the actors for acting, etc. It's up to you if you want to do that sort of thing but in the setting of a church service it might well get in the way and spoil the effect you're trying to produce. What I mean is subtler and more dramatic than that, and much more basic. It involves making sure what you put together leads into the middle and out again, so that the middle part of your play makes its proper impact - because that's where the action is.

The heart of any play is where you'd expect to find it: at the centre of the action. If, for instance, you were thinking about putting a play together about what happened at the first Easter you would design it so that the central part coincided with the crucifixion of Jesus. The play as a whole would be about Jesus' victory over death and its final message would be Resurrection. This would be in the last part, however - the final act - and in order to give this final part its full dramatic weight, the play *as a whole* would have to pivot on the cross. What I'm saying is, without the cross the resurrection would have a different meaning. The dramatic shape of any play on this theme of Easter must reproduce a story about going into death and rising from it again. Our play begins with Palm Sunday and ends with Easter Day. Between the two is the cross. You could write another story, using different events, even using different people, but you couldn't do it in a different way. Somehow or other it would always remind us of these things. For us, at Easter, the cross is crucial.

This is a very good example because it brings home something basic about drama. Drama is about conflict. This is what people mean when they talk about 'making a drama' about something. Plays, even the most lighthearted ones, always involve conflict of one kind or another. The drama of Easter is the greatest drama of all. It is the conflict between good and evil for the destiny of human beings everywhere and for all time. Conflict, however, is at the heart of every kind of play - conflict between individuals, cultures, ideas, purposes, states of mind, feelings, human needs. A play without any kind of conflict wouldn't be any kind of play at all. People in plays argue to put their point of view across, to evade charges made against them, to deny responsibility, to gain control of others, to get their own way. They argue out of one kind of difficulty and into another kind. They argue with themselves, in soliloquies, and with the audience to gain their support.

It's possible to argue too much, however, or at least to argue about too many things at once. A good play is one that knows how to stick to the point. Shakespeare's plays are clear examples of this. There may be several 'sub-plots', minor stories going on at the same time as the major one, but nobody is in any doubt where their attention should be focused. At the centre there is always an important human problem which always involves conflict. It may be treated comically or tragically or, as is often the case, with a mixture of both, but it is always what the play itself, the play as a whole, is *about*. You can't miss it. It hits you in the eye. Take *Romeo and Juliet*, for instance. The conflict here is between lovers who long to be together and their warring families, hell bent on tearing them apart. There are other things in the play: jealousies, rivalries, mistaken intentions, trials of strength, but the play has one main story and this is it. We call it the 'argument' of the play. Our job is not to get in its way. Whatever we do in drama, this is always something to bear in mind.

To sum up, the first thing about a play is this: it is something that really happens, not simply a visual aid but an actual event. A play is true if what happens in it is really like life, and only untrue if its message is false or distorted. The fact that it is *acted* is not the point. We're all of us acting a lot of the time; it's the way we live and communicate.

The second thing is this: the Christian faith always involves imagination. Holy Spirit uses our imagination to communicate with us. Drama is acted story and the Bible is full of stories, some of them actually told by Jesus. When we use drama, we are using the Bible's favourite way of getting things across to people.

Finally, this book isn't just about drama *in* worship. It is about drama *as* worship.

CHAPTER II: GETTING GOING

In a way this section should have come first, but the one about plays in general got in before it. After all, you can't have acting without a play to act in - not the kind of acting we're talking about, at least! On the other hand, it's the fact that people are 'terrified' to go on stage that stops some Christian groups doing any kind of drama, in church or anywhere else. So perhaps we'd better get down to basics straight away. What can you do if you've never acted before and want to start? If you want to get something across and the thought of acting scares you to death? What can you do?

To get down to things at a practical level. If you want to act, get yourself a director. If you want to direct, then you'll need actors. This may seem rather obvious but it has to be said right at the beginning. This is the nitty gritty. Actually it may not turn out quite like that, because directors often have to - or choose to - help out with the acting and actors find themselves taking part in the direction. Of the two alternatives, I favour the second rather than the first, because trying to act and direct at the same time is pretty hard work and I don't recommend it. Only do this if you really can't find somebody to take on a part and you've got a tight schedule (which often happens, although it shouldn't do. More about this later.). If you must slip in and take a role in the cast, make sure it's a small one. After all, Shakespeare himself played small parts in his own plays (not to mention Alfred Hitchcock!).

As long as everyone makes a firm decision to abide by the director's 'casting vote' there is no reason why the actors shouldn't help out with directing the play. The kind of drama which works best in churches comes from a real spirit of sharing. Whatever may go on in some amateur dramatic societies, and even professional companies, acting in church is a genuine group experience and stands or falls by this. If you want to show off, please go somewhere else. In this book we are considering groups of people who have come together specially to perform drama in church. They will be of different generations, experiences and levels of skill. Part of the joy in doing this kind of drama comes from overcoming these differences, and refusing to see them as difficulties. In the ordinary, down-to-earth setting of a church congregation these things are your raw material. You take what's there and start getting on with the job. If you work together as a group, sharing problems, encouraging one another, laughing about things that go wrong and finding out how to use everything that happens for the good of the drama and to build up your awareness of being part of what's going on, part of this new thing you're creating together, then the business of being, or having, a director isn't half as hard as you expected it to be. What's needed in these circumstances is a group-leader, not a theatre director.

There's plenty of work for the leader, however. Any group that gets together to do a play will have a mixed bag of things that people can and can't do - or at least think they can't do very well. For example, somebody will be keen but not particularly audible; someone else will have a lovely voice but difficulty in learning lines. Perhaps someone is very imaginative and yet painfully shy (a common one, this), or is overweight and therefore assumes (wrongly) that they have difficulty in appearing graceful. Each group is different from any other group. In drama you don't let this get in the way. Far from it, you make use of it! Differences are interesting. They are what drama is about.

The first basic rule in presenting a group play, then, is this: *Use what you've got.* Don't disguise things that don't seem to fit, but try to find a way of using them. Never, ever turn anybody away because you don't think they'll 'fit'. You need variety and contrast for this kind of drama: it's variety and contrast that make an immediate impact - and that's the kind of impact you must make here, because you have to be very different from what people expect to find in church, and yet completely relevant to what being a Christian means. So - use what you've got!

The second basic rule is: *Find the right material.* You must find out the kind of thing you want to act and stick to any decision you make. A lot of time can be spent making false starts and this tends to have a discouraging, and often divisive, effect on the group. Once you have arrived at an idea which appeals to you all, then start working.

As to the kind of things you might do, this depends on the kind of group you are, the nature of the occasion you're celebrating, the amount of time you have, the degree of experience of those taking part. We're concerned in this book with drama put on in church by members of the congregation itself, however, and this tends to narrow things down considerably. What we're likely to have in mind is something lasting less than half and hour and involving fewer than a dozen people, We shall be going on to look at ideas and themes for dramas which can be performed within a workshop setting in a later chapter. For the time being, I'm assuming that you won't be wanting to stage T.S. Eliot's *Murder in the Cathedral* or the Wakefield Mystery Plays. What we're looking for is something simpler, more direct, more spontaneous and personal, which will come across as belonging to a particular group of Christians because it bears the trade mark of the congregation that produced it. (If you haven't got a trade mark, then perhaps drama will help you get one!)

The third rule concerns rehearsing the play. The rule is: *Rehearse, rehearse, rehearse.* Take all the time you need and more. No matter how simple the drama, it needs to be perfectly rehearsed. Don't fall into the trap so many church groups lay themselves open to, and assume that because you're acting for friends they won't criticise you if you're not very good. Far from it - *because* they're your friends they won't see the need to pull their punches! If you want to go on acting in church, you have to get it right the first time or you'll be too discouraged to ever try it again. At least, you'll have to get it right *enough*. You'll have to show people you're really involved in what you're doing or you'll never convince them it's worth the effort. This is a matter of ten per cent inspiration and ninety per cent perspiration. A well-rehearsed show will have a much greater impact than one which depends on individual talent alone to make it work. However good individual actors are, it's the way an entire play hangs together that gets it across - and this means taking enough time to rehearse it properly. Once you've got it into shape, have at least two dress rehearsals where you run the whole thing through just as if the audience were there, without any stopping and starting. Remember, if it's drama in worship you may only have the chance to perform it once - so it really does have to be all right on the night, doesn't it?

Fourthly, *remember you are a group.* As actors you depend on one another and must try to help one another. This isn't as easy as it sounds - there's always a great deal of competition among actors, if only to get hold of the best parts. The level of commitment needed for this kind of group acting means that you can't allow this sort of thing to get in the way. There are bound to be differences of ability among you, but it's up to the best actors to make life as easy as possible for those who find it more difficult than they do. These are often people who have had to be persuaded to join in; they don't think of themselves as actors at all. If they are made to feel out of place their awkwardness will be obvious to the audience and the whole performance will suffer.

More importantly, they themselves will suffer. The fact is that acting groups only work properly if they pay attention to each other's strengths and weaknesses. Plays, like they used to say about wartime Atlantic convoys, 'move at the speed of the slowest ship'. You have to help one another. If you do it is amazing how people gain confidence and gaps in ability become much less noticeable. It's a case of "bearing one another's burdens". Christian groups shouldn't have to be reminded about it. And in fact nothing has so much impact in the theatre as a group of actors who care about each other.

And of course, about the audience. Point number five: *Remember the audience*. Audiences come first. Audiences are what drama is all about. There's really no chance you'll forget them, since you have to act in front of one. You may like acting - a lot of people do - but you won't enjoy having to go on stage. Nobody ever enjoys that. Seasoned professionals go weak at the knees at the prospect. Nothing binds a group together like having to face an audience, however kind and well-disposed the audience may be. So from that point of view there's little chance you'll forget them

On the other hand, even if you never actually manage to forget them, you have to train yourself to be able to ignore their presence once you're actually on stage. Being really involved in a play demands the highest degree of concentration on the part of the actors. This doesn't mean that you have to forget that they're there (that would be very difficult because of all the attention they are focusing on you), but it does mean you have to make sure they can always see and hear whatever is going on in the play. They must be able to do this for themselves. It is not the actors' job - not your job - to show them. Your job is to live in the play itself, trying to make it into something that is really happening, actually taking place, which they, the audience, are welcome to find out about. This should never be too easy otherwise you'll simply lose their interest. Nor should it be too difficult either or the same thing will happen. Sometimes actors leave the stage world they've been creating so that they can speak directly to the audience. This can be very effective. If you are in the audience being personally addressed like this by a member of the cast then it certainly strikes home. People who write and direct plays often use this technique. Again, it shouldn't be overdone or the surprise begins to wear off. And, of course, there must be an actual play taking place, a world of imagination created by the actors for them to be able to step 'out of frame' and talk to the audience head on, often to such good effect. We shall come back to ways of considering the audience's point of view later on when we consider speech and movement.

The sixth thing: *Where you're going to do it.* If you're going to do drama in church you will need to have the right kind of space. This doesn't mean that you need somewhere specially prepared and set aside for drama. What it does mean is that you have to be willing to make the very best of whatever space is available. Perhaps there's only one part of the church you can use; perhaps there's a lot of room and you can choose your vantage points. Whatever the case may be, what you have must be your starting place. In fact, working under difficulties of this kind can actually be an advantage; the kind of drama we're talking about always has an important element of surprise - let people see what you can make out of what's available. Flexibility and spontaneity are the name of the game!

It's a good idea to build up a repertoire of short, terse dramas you can put on anywhere and at any time in case you're invited to perform in other people's churches. For example, you can begin with a short dramatic idea and then develop it according to the circumstances. Here are two examples of the sort of thing I mean.

1   Enter a man, from the audience's left. He walks to the middle of the space, looks towards the back of the church (not at the audience). He consults his watch and exits right. Pause, and then: enter a woman from audience's right; she walks into the middle, looks over the heads of the audience to the back of the church, consults her watch and then exits left. What will happen next? It's over to you to decide. Whatever it is, you can count on having attracted the audience's attention.

2   Somebody walks into the acting space and puts a book down on the table that has been placed there. They leave. Somebody else enters the scene from another direction. They take the book off the table, open it and start to read. They start to get interested and move out of the scene, reading as they go. The first person returns in a businesslike way to fetch his book. It isn't there so he looks round for it. Suddenly he sees the audience. Does he speak to them? Doesn't he? What happens next?

3   Somebody arrives in front of the audience. They have a dog on a lead, or a wheelbarrow, or a pram. In fact they can have whatever they like, because the audience can't see it. They, for their part, don't seem to be able to see the audience either, except for one member of it sitting on the front row whom they greet enthusiastically. They are eager to show them what it is they are leading, pushing or carrying. They do this in detail, without saying what it actually is.

These are three off the cuff examples of potentially dramatic situations from which short plays can be developed. The acting exercises we will be looking at later on can also be used like this. Another reason why I have included them here is because they demonstrate ways in which a play can begin without needing a conventional stage with curtains, proscenium arch, special lighting etc. Plays have a life of their own: they take over any space that happens to be available.

CHAPTER III: SOME ACTING BASICS

First of all, these really are basics. There are some things everybody has to remember about acting, whether they consider themselves to be 'real' actors or not. If you follow these ground rules, you may consider yourself to be a real actor because you'll have learned the basic job of an actor, which is to let the play speak through you. It doesn't matter whether you have made the play up or taken it out of a book, "the play's the thing." It, not you, is the point of the exercise.

A Can you see me?

So first of all you must be visible. If you have powerful stage lighting you'll need stage make-up or your faces will look washed out and two-dimensional. If you settle for the ordinary church lighting, however, heavy make-up will make you look 'stagey' and you are much better off without it. The play must take place where it can be clearly seen by everybody. This has already been mentioned in the last section. Some things may seem obvious but should nevertheless be said. For example, always make sure nobody has decided to stand right in front of you, and remember not to stand in front of anyone else. This doesn't mean you have to stand in line abreast across the acting area. There are all sorts of ways you can group yourselves; long lines can be boring anyway. (You can forget the old fashioned piece of advice about not standing with your back to the audience. If you never do this, you'll never be able to turn and face them, will you? And this is a very expressive thing to do.) Contrasts are usually more exciting than things that are neatly balanced; except when something has been carefully arranged to stand out in the middle of chaos. Similarly, disorder draws attention when everything around is neat and tidy - an overturned chair in a tidy sitting room demonstrates immediately where the action is. The place where people stand in relation to each other on stage shows precisely that; in other words it reveals their relationships within the play as well as how they are feeling at the point in the story they have reached. Sometimes you may find you can express more by where you stand and how and when you alter your position on stage than you can by actually speaking. Movements can speak louder than words: their meaning is clear and unmistakable.

As to speaking on stage - well, you obviously need to speak louder than you do in ordinary conversation. You also have to speak more clearly. In fact, this means speaking more slowly than usual. To begin with, this has to be done quite systematically because nervousness will make you speak faster than usual, and you have to be aware of this and slow yourself down.

Although they like to see your face, the audience doesn't necessarily need to see it head-on. People don't stand side by side to talk to each other, and you needn't either. This is a rule of the worn-out ways of doing theatre. Try to face the person you're talking to by standing at right angles to the front of the acting area. When you look at what's going on up-stage or turn to take in the audience you'll have to make a definite movement, either of your head or your whole body, and this will capture the attention of the audience and make your performance more real, more immediate. When you make a movement on stage, let it be for a definite purpose; don't drift into the acting area, enter in order to do something definite - fetch a book, put a cup on the table, pull something imaginary etc. Whatever it is you do will hold people's attention so long as it is done with clarity and definition.

And so long as it doesn't distract from what someone else is trying to do or say. This is really important. The worst thing you can do on stage is to take the audience's attention from whatever it is they should be looking at and listening to and fasten it on yourself. Never, never do this. It is called 'distracting' (at least that's its polite name), and it takes some people a long time and lot of persistence to learn how to stop doing it. When someone else has a long speech or during a time of stillness, or simply when you feel that people in the audience aren't taking as much notice of you as you'd like them to do - these are times when the demon strikes and you start to fill the gap by straightening your tie or tapping your foot or trying out your range of interesting facial expressions. All that happens, though, is that a dramatic scene is ruined and a fellow actor made very angry indeed.

Movement needs practice. Simply walking across the acting area seems strange at first. Practise doing it normally and easily as if you're simply engaged on your own business, whatever it may be. Then practise moving and speaking at the same time; then moving quickly whilst speaking slowly, and vice versa. You'll find this hard to do, however it's something well worth practising. Everyone does it quite naturally in real life when they aren't thinking about it. Get to do it easily on stage too.

Learn to stand still. This isn't only so that you'll stop fidgeting and distracting from the scene. It's because you need to know all the things you can express without speech and movement, simply by posture. Practise expressing feelings, intentions, states of mind by the way you're standing, sitting, kneeling or lying down. Then start to change the way you're feeling by thinking about something else and see if your body wants to shift position as your mind changes. Explore the way in which your posture and bodily attitude change in accordance with your state of mind - and what's even more interesting, how your state of mind changes when your body starts to express something else. Acting isn't only about ideas and feelings which are expressed in words; it's about the ways in which you reveal yourself in your physical and mental presence; you as a whole person, living and moving amongst other people who aren't just minds but bodies as well.

One way of doing this is called 'sculpting'. You reproduce an idea or a feeling or a state of mind by the way you stand or move. Somebody puts you in a position expressing something, or you put yourself into it, just as a sculptor makes a statue out of a block of stone or a lump of clay. You can take this a stage further by building up corporate sculpts to express how you feel as a group, rather like the statue of the Burghers of Calais in the riverside park by the Houses of Parliament in London. Notice, I have to give clear directions where this is, in case you haven't seen it. If you have, you'll know exactly what I'm talking about because the statue has such an impact on the beholder. This is why sculpting is such a vivid way of getting things across. Unlike statues carved out of stone, however, yours can move; this means that people can group themselves to demonstrate the reality of a situation which affects them all in different ways and then gradually move into a posture which shows that things have now changed, changing their lives in the process. A group sculpt can move from tragedy to deliverance, sadness to joy, anger to forgiveness, enmity to reconciliation, war to peace, without actually moving from one part of the acting area to another. The living picture transforms itself as bodies uncurl, hands lift, people revive as hope re-enters the world. And, of course, the opposite can happen, as the group moves from a joyful stance to one expressing sorrow, or one of hope to one of despair. Group sculpts are a kind of mini-theatre, a bodily shorthand for dramatic ideas. They owe their power to communicate to the fact that nothing is actually said. The spectator has to draw his or her own conclusions. Such sculpts and other kinds of acting without words are a good way of discovering how effective movement itself can be.

B Can you hear me?

The answer to this is usually no! It just isn't enough to speak in a play the same way as you would normally do in an ordinary conversation. This doesn't mean you have to put on a special 'actor's voice', making different sorts of sounds from the ones you normally produce - unless, that is, you are playing a character who speaks in a different way from you; perhaps somebody from another country or county or district from yours. What it does mean, though, is that you have to speak loudly and clearly enough to be heard properly at one end of the church when you're standing at the other. And you must learn to do this without shouting. Actors are trained to speak in ways that seem normal and ordinary, but are specially designed to be heard at a distance. To do this properly takes a great deal of practice. However the underlying principle is straightforward. When we want to talk in a way that can be heard some way off, we tend to tighten our throat muscles and force the sound through them so that it will have more impact. The result is a strained and slightly abrasive sound which doesn't actually travel very well and sooner or later results in a sore throat. If we relax our chest and throat muscles, however, we leave a clear passage for air to be drawn upwards and outwards by our diaphragm which acts as a powerful bellows to produce all the volume we need to be heard at the back of the church. The secret is *relaxation;* learning to stand, move and speak without muscle tension.

There is a psychological aspect to this as well. We are easier to hear if we have a mental image of the people we want to communicate with. This means that if you think about the people sitting at the very back of the church and *speak as if you are addressing them,* the odds are that you will be heard loud and clear, without ever feeling you need to shout. Always remember that clarity and articulation are more important than volume. Consonants are crucial because they distinguish one word from another whereas vowel sounds can easily merge together. *T, k, d, g, p* all need practice; so choose a passage with lots of them in it and rehearse saying it as clearly and precisely as you can - and do it from the diaphragm not from the throat! For quality of tone, try using the vowels, chanting each of them either on one note or on an ascending or descending scale. Never be self conscious about this; being heard is a serious business and deserves to have some time spent on it. Before you begin to act, both voice and body always need loosening up. You'll find this has a relaxing effect on your state of mind, too.

Being heard isn't only a matter of volume and clarity, how loudly and clearly you produce sounds. It has also to do with what we actually say when we do speak. Usually when we're speaking quite normally, without having specially prepared what we're going to say, we make perfectly good sense. The problems occur when we're reading aloud or repeating things we have learned by heart. I don't mean that we just gabble them off without thinking what they're supposed to express, although we've all done this at some time in our lives: I mean the way we read and recite when we're grown up and should know better.

You may decide not to use words at all in your drama, and simply rely on movement and gesture to establish what you want to say. As we saw, this can be a very effective way of working. If, however, you do have lines:

(1) Try to say them as if you haven't learned them. Don't recite them, say them as if you were really speaking to a real person. The fact that you know beforehand what you're

going to say shouldn't affect the directness and simplicity of the way you say it. Try to talk naturally as you usually do. Don't 'say the line', speak to a person. Similarly, when you're actually reading something aloud - perhaps it's Sunday and your turn to read the lesson - react to it as if the message it contains is as new to you, to *all* of you, as it was to the people who heard it for the very first time.

(2) Try to stress the right words in any sentence. By the 'right' words I mean the ones that carry most of the meaning. These are usually either verbs or nouns, actions and experiences, or people and things. Again, this depends on the meaning of what you are saying; but it also determines whether or not it will have any meaning at all. Take this sentence, for instance: *John and Mary went into the house.* The meaning is quite obvious; you don't have to stress anything to get it across. If you did stress any of the words in this sentence they would be 'John' and 'Mary' (either *John* and *Mary* or *John and Mary*), 'went' and 'house'. People would need to know who you are talking about, what it was they did, and what they did it to. If you've just been talking about Mary and John you don't need to put any emphasis on their names - although they must still be clear and audible; the same is true of 'house'. It is also true of 'went into' - so long as going into the house is a perfectly ordinary thing for this couple to do. If you're mentioning John and Mary for the first time, and their going into the house is important for the story you are telling, then of course you emphasise the appropriate words: *John* and *Mary went into the house.* This is all quite straightforward. It's worth mentioning, however, because the kind of thing this or any sentence means depends very largely on the emphasis, or lack of it, that each word

28

receives. People sometimes get into bad habits. Sometimes it's people who should know better. News readers, for example, often fall into the temptation to 'hit' the first word or the opening phrase in each sentence before hurrying on to begin the next one. I suppose there's some excuse for this; there always seems to be more news to deliver than time to deliver it in. What is stranger, and much more annoying, is the fashion for stressing prepositions at the expense of the nouns they refer to: John and Mary went *into* the house (or *round* the corner, or *through* the wood, or *to* the fish and chip shop). If this habit allows other words to be deprived of the proper emphasis needed to get the particular meaning of a sentence across, it is an important point.

(3) Try not to let your voice drop at the end of a line. The last words of a sentence are often the most important ones - we want to know what happened! If you listen to some railway station announcers you'll notice how their voices drop at the end of each announcement. The volume stays the same but the pitch alters. It's as if they were singing a tune that stays on the same note and then goes down a note to end with. This is not how people usually say things. We speak directly in order to get our meaning across, except when our pitch rises because we're asking a question.

(4) Try not to speak too quickly. If you're nervous you tend to press on more rapidly in order to get it over with. Remember to slow down. Take a moment before you go on stage to collect yourself. If you actually want to speak quickly, because it's right for the play, you must practise doing so without tripping over what you have to say. As a general rule, however, inexperienced actors tend to speak too fast to begin with.

C Come and join us

I said that actors must be clearly seen and heard. Now I want to say that they have to be inconspicuous and unobtrusive, too. This seems an obvious contradiction - how can you be both things at once? Well you can't - so I'd better find another way of putting it. I mean, of course, that *characters in plays* should be clearly visible and audible, so that the actors playing the parts don't get in the way. Actors must learn to imagine that they are the people they are pretending to be, so that they don't get in the way of the drama. You can never lose yourself completely so that you're completely submerged by the part you're playing. It's a good thing you can't do this or you wouldn't be able to pay attention to the other things you have to remember - like being audible, not distracting attention from anyone else and recognising your cues when they come up. At the same time, your main job as an actor is to let the audience see the play itself rather than you performing the play.

This is largely a matter of attitude of mind. In Shakespeare's *King Henry V* the Chorus invited the audience to enjoy the play by sharing the actors' imaginative re-telling of the story: "Let us ...

> On your imaginary forces work.
> Suppose within the girdle of these walls
> Are now confined two mighty monarchies ...
> ... Into a thousand parts divide one man
> And make imaginary puissance."

Acting is about pretending *together.* The poet and critic, Samuel Taylor Coleridge of *Ancient Mariner* fame, described the audience's share of the bargain as "a willing suspension of disbelief". What this means is that the audience, by their willingness to share in the imaginary world created by the actors, have already undertaken their part of the bargain. They have done this by agreeing to be an audience.

You see how this fits in with what we have been saying about acting? You don't only have to be careful not to get in the way of the other actors; you have to train yourself not to get in the way of the play itself. Or rather, not to obstruct the audience's attempts to share in the imaginative experience which is drama. There are several ways you can do this. The most obvious of them is quite simply not knowing your lines!

Learning lines is a chore, but it has to be done. There's no easy way round. In fact, the worst thing about acting isn't having to go on-stage; that may be terrifying but it usually goes off quickly once you've made the plunge. Learning lines never gets much easier; and as you get older it definitely becomes harder. Unless you have a lot of rehearsals and the play you are in runs for a great many performances, you can never really relax in the knowledge that you're word perfect. Actors find they have to keep on running over their lines at odd moments of the day, whenever they have the chance. This is the real hard work of acting.

Fortunately, the kind of plays we're talking about in this book don't usually have all that many lines, and some may not have any at all. So, whatever lines there are there's no excuse for not knowing them. The secret is to know the play itself. Get to know it well, so you really understand why things happen the way they do, and why you say what you have to say. Don't simply learn the lines mentally, learn them *physically* as well - do the movements that go with the words. The movements will remind you of the story; you'll remember what happens to the character you are playing and *why* they say what they do. When you've got this far, you'll find that remembering the actual words is much easier. Don't bother if people think you must be going a bit mad, walking around and talking to yourself. By building your scene for yourself like this, you tie words in with actions, and both these things with the feelings behind them.

Crossing the room, putting down milk for the cat, replacing a book in the bookcase, all remind you of what you're feeling and thinking while you do these things - and what you say as a result. Try this approach: you'll find it works better than simply repeating the lines parrot fashion until you think you're word perfect. And you'll be too much involved in the play to get in the way of it.

The other thing that gets in the way of the play is an actor who refuses to be part of the team so that he or she persists in giving a solo performance. Because everyone else is working together and this actor holds aloof, everything she or he does stands out against the background of the rest of the play, like a pop star with a backing group. Apart from annoying the rest of the cast this always upsets the balance of the play. It becomes less of a play and more of a solo performance. You have to be very skilful indeed to carry it off; if a bad actor does it the effect is catastrophic. The point is, however, that not even a very good actor can do this and really get away with it. Every individual part depends on every other and everyone must be involved in what is happening to the same degree. To distort one role at the expense of the others is to distort the whole play. I once saw a famous actor play a star role in one of Ibsen's plays. It was supposed to be a realistic glimpse of suburban life, but somehow he managed to make it a showcase for his own talents. Unfortunately, the play suffered. Because of him it lost its ordinariness. He was the star - and he got in the way.

Obviously, other things can get in the way too: things you haven't planned for and don't expect. Like the lighting failing or the scenery starting to fall down. These things happen. They're particularly likely to do so when you're performing in a building that wasn't designed for plays - like a church, for instance. Never try and ignore them or pretend they're not happening. If you notice something has gone really wrong, you may be sure the audience has noticed it too. It's a chance you can't afford to take - because if they know things have gone wrong and think that *you* know and won't let on, then the spell is broken. At the same time, if you admit this fact to the audience you can use it as an opportunity to renew your contract with them about suspending their disbelief. Look what has happened, you can say. Please accept our apologies and we'll carry on with the play, shall we?

Of course, if the hitch is only slight it isn't worth making all this fuss about it. Lots of things go wrong on-stage and the audience never notice. Or if they do they think it's part of the play. So here's another rule - whatever you do on stage, try to do it with conviction. You'd be surprised how many minor mistakes actors get away with by being given the benefit of the doubt. But if the mistake is obvious you're much better owning up to it one way or another. (Sometimes it's possible to acknowledge the unexpected without actually coming out of character to do it. I remember a production in which the set literally fell down on the actors. One of them was in the middle of a telephone conversation at the time. He didn't turn a hair, but simply adjusted the script to fit the new situation: "I'm afraid I have to ring off now, my dear: the old place is falling down round our ears!")

So what sort of conclusion can we draw from all this? One thing stands out: 'sharing' and 'showing' are different from each other. A sharing drama isn't a showing drama. There may be times in a sharing drama where the aim is simply to demonstrate something to the audience, but the play itself is *participation* rather than *demonstration*. This calls for a particular state of mind on the part of the actors, a positive intention to involve the audience in what they themselves have in hand. In the kind of drama that creates the best response from a congregation in church, everybody present plays an important part, not simply the actors. From an acting point of view this means being willing to *let the audience in,* to give them the opportunity to discover the drama for themselves. As Joan Littlewood used to say: "Let them do the work." Let them experience the play not merely receive it. In order to experience something in a way which has a real effect on us, a lasting effect, we ourselves must be allowed to make some of the effort involved. We must be presented with the problem before receiving the answer or we will never go so far as to work anything out for ourselves. Once we have started to work things out, however, we're as good as hooked: we'll stick with the investment we have made until it pays a dividend.

How does this affect acting? Probably more than you'd think, although it mainly concerns experienced actors. Joan's advice is for people who really enjoy acting and who try to give the part everything they've got. Be careful, she would say, try not to give it *too much.* This isn't a case of ordinary over-acting, which usually means exaggeration for dramatic effect and stands out to an audience as simply un-real; an actor who overacts is always very obviously an actor, albeit a bad one. But it is possible to identify so closely with the character you are playing that you leave the audience out of the picture altogether - or rather, you hand them the situation on a plate: This is precisely how I feel, take it or leave it. If you really want to get the audience interested in how your character feels - if you want them to care how he or she feels - you would do much better if you weren't so 'up front' about it. As Arthur Miller said, "Just play the text, not what it reminds you of!" Stand back and let it remind *them.*

Here's an example of what I mean. Mr Zero in Elmer Rice's play *The Adding Machine* has been in love with his assistant, Daisy Diana Devore for thirty years. On the occasion of the

Office Outing when the two of the them are riding along on a hay-cart, he takes her by surprise by saying, quite suddenly, "Gee, I love you." There is only one way to say this line: it must be said straightforwardly, in a matter of fact way, loudly but without stressing any of the words more than the others. The circumstances under which Mr Zero says this, the fact that it is the first time in thirty years he has ever said it and has never dreamed he would ever say it, must not affect how the line is actually said. The actor has only one task here: on no account must he allow his feelings, the feelings he has developed as Mr Zero, get in the way of the play. So he closes his mind to what is going on and simply says the line. Maybe he thinks of something else while he's saying it. The emotion, when it comes, belongs to the audience, who greet what he says with a tidal wave of feeling. If he had played the line in another way they could be saying: Look, what a brilliant actor - look what he's going through! As it is, all they can say is: Poor man. Poor Zero.

That is letting an audience feel. Letting them find out for themselves what is going on. The secret is, of course, that you can only do this sort of thing if you really feel for the character you're playing - if you feel enough for him or her as to know how she or he would feel if such and such were to happen to them. In this case this meant understanding the kind of person Zero was, not at all the kind of person to say things like that. Feel them, yes: say them, no. The danger is that we should let our feelings about him affect the way in which he would naturally communicate, and so stop him communicating in his own way - the way the audience found so moving.

Acting is learning how to feel and behave *as if* we were someone else, not as if someone else were us. It involves judgement and restraint as well as the ability to feel. But without that ability there is no drama at all.

D Some Acting Games

These are ways of practising acting and getting used to the idea of using drama to express yourself. They can be used as a way of warming-up before a rehearsal or an actual performance. On the whole they aren't very serious, because laughter is a good way to relax, and being relaxed helps you concentrate on the play. So if these games make you laugh, you're probably playing them the right way.

1 Group Song

The group choose a song which they can all sing, and sing it all together before every rehearsal and performance. The song should be light-hearted but not ridiculous (or you won't be able to sing the song for laughing). It should have an adventurous air to it and stress the group solidarity and the joint nature of whatever you've undertaken to do together. It can be made up or borrowed from elsewhere. Ideally it should have a simple accompaniment of the kind that can be performed without an instrument, so that half the group can sing the melody while the others vocalise the tune. Then you can swap over and sing it again, as many times as you want.

2 Breakfast with Wotsisname

This is a simple mimed game in which each member of the group goes through the stages of getting up in the morning, washing, visiting the loo, dressing, having breakfast and going off to work. She or he does this by using the others as 'props' in order to set the scene: two people become the bed, two more a wardrobe, one a teapot, one a toast rack etc. There probably won't be enough people to go round, but even if there are, people are encouraged to swap roles and try out other impersonations - a wash basin doubling as a telephone, or a lamp-stand as a toothbrush, for example. The more serious you are about this the funnier it gets.

3 Battle of Names

The group stands in a circle and each member says his or her name in turn. When the circle of names is complete the process starts again. This time each person is allowed to say the name of the person standing beside her or him, *either to the left or right.* The names go backwards and forwards as people either resist by saying the name of a neighbour who has said *their* name or 'go with the flow' by saying the name of the person on the other side. No matter who plays this game, interesting exchanges take place. Only names are spoken but they can, of course, be said a whole range of ways -authoritatively, pleadingly, mournfully, aggressively, sexily etc. etc. Sometimes pairs of players address and re-address each other over and over again in a battle of wills as to which of them will give in, trying to bludgeon or cajole, dominate or seduce. There's endless opportunity for acting even though (or perhaps because) you can only use one word at a time.

A similar exercise involves pairs of people who carry out a dialogue using numbers instead of words. Only three numbers (1, 2 and 3) may be used and must be used consecutively:

> **Person A** — 'one'
> **Person B** — 'two'
> **Person A** — 'three'
> **Person B** — 'one'
> **Person A** — 'two'
> **Person B** — 'three'
> **Person A** — 'one'
> **Person B** — 'two'   etc.

Players may use three different sounds or gestures instead of numbers.

This looks very easy but is in fact quite tricky and needs concentration. It helps develop the ability to listen properly to the message you are receiving from someone else, rather than simply thinking about what you yourself are going to say next. What you have to say obviously depends on what is said to you. This game keeps *you* on your toes!

4 Not *me!*

This is a real acting game, where a dramatic situation is set up and played through. It's a very simple drama, however, revolving round a Master (or Mistress) and his (or her) servants. The Mistress (or Master) accuses one of the servants of some or other relatively minor offence - having done this or not done that - and the servant denies it, blaming a colleague, somebody slightly lower in the domestic hierarchy. This is a story familiar to anyone who knows (a) the New Testament, (b) Shakespeare's plays. It can be played in different ways and at different speeds, seriously or light-heartedly. It is about dominance and submission, social systems and personal relationships. What makes it dramatic, however, is that it is about conflict and (eventual) resolution.

Master: I put my book on this table. I put it here last night. Where is it?
Servant 1 (turning to Servant 2): Did you move that book? (etc.)
Servant 2 (to Servant 3): Where did you put that book? (etc.)
Servant 3 (to Servant 4): Come on, give it back! I'm surprised at you! (etc.)
(Servant 4 takes the book she/he has been reading and gives it to Master.)
Master: This isn't it. This isn't the one I mean. It's the wrong book!
Servant 4 (to Servant 3): It isn't the right one. Why did you give me the *wrong* book? (etc.)
Servant 3 (to Servant 2): You know that book you gave me ... (etc.)
Servant 2 (to Servant 1): I suppose you thought giving me that book was *funny.* (etc.)

And so on. How it ends, and how many servants are included is up to you. As this is a game, you can have as many as you want, involving everyone present. If it was a real play the optimal number of servants would be three because that is the number of climax and completeness. You could have as many incidents involving a succession of three people, things or events as you like.

5 Railway Carriage

Two travellers, strangers, sitting opposite each other in an otherwise empty carriage (one of the old fashioned compartment type carriages, not the modern kind with a corridor running down the middle). The two people should be as different from each other as possible (a miner and a female Tory MP; a farmer and a computer programmer; an Indian doctor and a punk). The dialogue is extemporised and the subject matter left open so that the differences between the two people can be exaggerated to taste. At one point, however, real contact must be made; one of them says something which strikes a chord for the other, and the tone of the conversation changes, becoming less cautious and more personal. Recognition of a kindred spirit begins to supplant people's natural defensiveness in the face of the unknown and potentially threatening. The outcome can be funny or moving, according to how the game is played. Quite often it ends in one person recognising the other as a long-lost relative.

Other settings may be used for the same basic situation. Those who are familiar with the film *Brief Encounter* feel constrained to move in another direction altogether and develop something powerful and sensitive out of what is, after all, another example of the original human drama: being alive in a world with other people in it, and suddenly coming face to face with this fact.

6 Magic Shop

This is an acting game in which people play different roles without actually adopting different characters. It is an exercise in using drama to look at personal meanings and human values.

I've included it because it can be adapted for use in church settings. Basically only two people need to be involved: the Magic Shop Shopkeeper and the Customer. The procedure is extremely simple. Customer enters Shopkeeper's shop. He or she is greeted by Shopkeeper who tells them that the shop is Magic because it has in stock anything and everything anybody could ever ask for. Customer takes advantage of this and asks for his or her heart's desire. Shopkeeper replies that this request can be granted. It must be paid for, however. Customer asks what he or she can give in exchange. Shopkeeper answers that in the interests of fair trading it must be something Customer thinks is of equal value, something Customer already possesses.

The game can only have one of two outcomes. Either Customer decides that what they want is worth paying a very high price for, or they decide to hold on to what they have, in which case they depart, disappointed of the chance to live dangerously but relieved that nothing appears to be lost. In either case, the game gives rise to a lot of self-examination and this involves a re-assessment of personal values - what is the most precious thing I possess?

In this game people ask for whatever they want - some for material things like a coveted sports car or a win on the National Lottery; others want to be more attractive, cleverer, less self-indulgent. Many simply ask for happiness. When I have played it in church people from the congregation have made requests for others as well as themselves. It has given people an opportunity to share one another's burdens. In the atmosphere of worship and devotion we considered what was most important to us - what belonged to our fulfilment as children of God and brothers and sisters of one another.

The game is really about the price of commitment. Exactly what are we willing to give up in order to serve God and add to

His glory? The Magic Shopkeeper's question - What would you be willing to abandon in order to secure the thing you value most? - and his refusal to sell that most precious of things short by demanding less than its personal worth reminds Christians of Jesus' recommendation to the young man who wanted to attain the Kingdom of God: Sell all you have, and follow me. Follow me and receive more than you knew how to ask for.

7 Hollywood

This is a rather misleading name because the scope of this game is much wider than cinema, and takes in stage, television, opera, ballet, puppets, Punch and Judy, any and every kind of dramatic presentation. This breadth of scope is, in fact, the whole point. The group invents a story that can be acted in a single scene, then it divides into two smaller groups, each of which rehearses the scene using a particular style of acting and/or presentation. When both teams are ready they take turns acting out their mini-dramas to each other so that each drama is performed to an audience. The point about this game, however, is that the team can decide to act and present their drama in any style they want. Typical acting styles would be: melodrama, Shakespearean (or Greek) tragedy, Whitehall (or Aldwych) farce, cartoon characters, puppets.

A variation of 'Hollywood' involves experimenting with speeds rather than styles. Teams divide up and present their dramas to each other; this time, however, the same scenario is played at three contrasting speeds - normal, as slow as possible and then very fast. (It should be pointed out that this game always makes people laugh and has been known to end in a certain amount of chaos!)

8 Do you remember ...

People remember things that they have all experienced and

act them out. This, too, works best when the group is divided up in order to form two casts and two audiences. Each cast spends some time finding a subject which (a) refers to everybody's life story, and (b) can be dramatised easily. This doesn't have to be anything which has had a big effect on people's lives. It doesn't need to be serious at all, in fact. But it must be something shared by everyone taking part. If it rings a few bells in the audience too, that will be all the better.

9 Surprise Surprise

The last game was about things you recognise, memories you share. This game is about surprises. Both these things - what you know and are familiar with and what you don't know because you never expected it - are an essential part of drama. Drama is about the unexpected and surprising, and you can't be surprised unless you were expecting something else, can you? Greek tragedies involved what they called *peripeteia,* a dramatic reversal of fate, the point at which the story changed direction, 'turning round on itself' (which is what the word *peripeteia* means). This is such an important feature of drama that it has to be present not only in tragedy but in every kind of play. Somewhere or other there is an element of shock, whether it is shockingly funny or shockingly sad. Shock may seem a strange word to use because we associate it with things like horror movies and so-called 'adult' videos. But this is only one use of the word: we can actually be disturbed by things which are not 'shocking' in themselves but are made so by the circumstances in which they happen; things that disturb our equilibrium in one way or another, whether to make us laugh or cry or simply understand something we thought we knew about and suddenly find we didn't. Well not in that way, at least.

This kind of thing grows out of the drama itself as you begin to put it together. I don't think people usually write plays by thinking of something surprising, a dramatic reversal of some kind, and then writing a play to fit it (although I'm sure it must sometimes be done like that). In plays put together by groups, dramatic situations tend to grow out of the way situations evolve and characters interact with one another. Which is why making up scenarios and plots revolving round or leading up to a big surprising event is a very useful kind of acting game to practise. When you have to start thinking about the drama you're going to do in church before a congregation, you may remember some of the situations you experimented with when you were using members of your own group as a stand-in audience. If you can surprise them, you're on your way!

10 Give me a line

This is a game about what actors call 'building a character'. Sometimes you may be asked to play the part of somebody very like yourself, but usually actors are faced with having to impersonate a different kind of person altogether. This isn't the basic thing about acting. The most important aspect of the art is even more obvious - imagining that what you are pretending to be happening actually is happening. As an actor you have to imagine that a situation which somebody has made up is actually real and that you yourself are somehow involved in it. Only then do you get round to imagining that you are involved not as yourself but as *somebody else*. Actually, the first part is harder than the second: if you can imagine being involved, you can somehow imagine being someone else - maybe not at first, but after you have practised it enough.

At first, however, the part you have got to play seems too different from you. You can understand how somebody like that might feel, but how would they show their feelings; how would they move, stand, sit, speak and generally present themselves? What would they be *like*? One of the ways actors get to grips with this is by settling on something which they feel would be typical of the character they're going to play. Sometimes they call this 'getting a line on the character'. Anything may spark this process off - a hat, a pipe, a characteristic turn of phrase or way of walking, a particular taste in clothes; anything can form the nucleus of a character you can imagine clearly enough to impersonate 'from the inside' - that is, with sympathy and understanding.

You can make a useful game out of this by choosing one of a selection of objects, garments, tones of voice or turns of phrase, and letting your imagination revolve around it. Let yourself experiment with it, as if you're trying it out for size. Think about it in a constructive way, play games with it, ask yourself what it reminds you of, what you feel you would do with it. Then go on to think about the person who might own or use something like this. What might they themselves be like? Can you picture them at all? Now start trying out your picture by talking, walking, standing, sitting like the individual whose image has begun to develop in your imagination and now starts to emerge as a real character. When everyone has created a character in this way, you can invent a drama involving them all.

These are a few suggestions about preparing to put on drama in church by playing theatre games amongst yourselves. The more of this kind of thing you can do the better, because it helps you to get a good basic grasp on what drama and theatre are really about. So keep an eye open for useful approaches because you never know what you might be able to use when it comes to it, and the moment comes when you must get down to the real job of play-making. So carry on inventing!

Chapter IV: Putting Drama Together

When I was writing my notes for this chapter I forgot to cross my 't's' in 'putting' so that, looking back, I found I had written *pulling* instead. In a way, that would have been better. Making plays is always to do with pulling things (and people) together. Just being dramatic about a lot of things doesn't make a play, although people often seem to think it does. Even a very short sketch should be carefully constructed so that it makes its point in as effective a way as possible. Plays are the very opposite of those old fashioned sermons in which the preacher drones on until everyone is half asleep: "And seventhly ..." I think that a good sermon makes one point. The preacher may lead up to it by saying other things as well, but the purpose of these is to draw attention to the main thing that he or she wants to get across. Good preachers only use material which will contribute to the central message of the sermon, carefully selecting ideas and stories which either by corroboration or contrast are evidence in support of the case being presented. A good preacher works very like a barrister, trained to use all available resources to convince a jury of the weight of the arguments supporting whatever it is that he is trying to establish.

A The Magic Number Three

The kind of thing you were experimenting with when you were thinking about dramatic situations and making up acting games to try them out in has to be pulled together to make a real play. I'm not just thinking about plays that come in three or even five acts and last for two and a half hours. Everything from a stand-up comedian's spiel to a full-sized play needs ordering, directing, fining down, *focusing*. For one thing, as we saw earlier, they all need a suitable beginning, middle and end, so that you can "tell 'em you're going to do (say, show, reveal) it, do it and tell 'em you've done it." Euclid, the Greek geometrician-philosopher, said that three is the number of perfection precisely because it not only has a beginning, middle and end, it actually is a beginning, a middle and an end. This is why it carries such conviction: something said in three stages is well said. As Lewis Carroll said in *The Hunting of the Snark:* "What I tell you three times is true." (You can draw your own theological conclusions about this!) Events are arranged in succession not showed simultaneously. This doesn't mean that you have to present everything in chronological order: you're allowed to choose the order you think best suits your purpose in saying what you, the playwright, want to say. Your play, your order; but the shape will stay the same.

It's the third blow that finally crushes, the third son that wins the hand of the princess, the third casket that contains the letters. It's the third wish that rebounds to restore the status quo, the audience laugh the third time they hear the comedian's catchphrase. Three is the number of completeness both in the sense of reaching a climax and that of restoring the tension that one and two have created between themselves. Three establishes and restores; two may signal a dramatic confrontation but only three can really make a point. Only three can make a *play,* by pulling its parts together properly and making it genuinely dramatic.

B One thing at a time

As I said, plays present events one after another rather than all at once. So does putting them together. Let's have a look at this from the beginning.

You decide, as a group, that you would like to do some drama in church. Perhaps somebody has made the suggestion and the idea has grown, and now you're getting down to it. You may or may not have actually chosen a group leader. At this

46

stage, perhaps, you want to talk things over together as a group. There are some things that can be decided first of all:

a) You have a basic choice about the purpose of doing drama in church: are you going to tailor your drama to fit the church service or the church service to fit the drama? If you decide to do the second you may go on to perform the play you have chosen to do (or the one you intend to make up for yourselves) in the way you choose to do it. The service will take second place, with hymns and prayers, perhaps even a sermon, on the themes expressed in the play. If this is what you want to do, then go ahead. Remember, however, that if the play is going to be the main item, you don't need much of anything else or the event will become unwieldy. And please, *please* do tell the congregation beforehand: they will be upset if they arrive expecting a service and are treated to a play instead. An awful lot depends on what people are expecting, remember! However, I'm assuming that you will probably choose the first option and try to design a drama for the service rather than the other way round. If you do, the rest of these instructions apply directly to you.

b) You must decide what kind of dramatic approach to use. There are several ways of thinking about this. To put it as simply as possible, drama involves two basic ingredients: sound and movement. You can remain stationary and speak (or sing, of course); you can speak (sing) and move around; or you can move around in silence. These will be your three basic options. It goes without saying that if you neither move nor make any sound you will soon lose your audience's attention. Each of these three approaches can be effectively dramatic. Usually actors move and speak or move and sing; but I have often seen drama in which those taking part speak to one another and to the audience without actually moving from their positions, which may be all

47

together, as in a 'group sculpt' or stationed in various parts of the church at various distances from one another. In dance sequences and mimed dramas, of course, everybody moves but nobody speaks at all! You can do any of these things so long as it's clear to the audience/congregation what you are doing; which means that you should be careful not to try and do them all at once or there will be only confusion and annoyance, a sense of wires being crossed.

c) If you decide to speak, are you going to learn your lines, improvise them or actually read them aloud from the script? Although it can be quite effective to read lines (and so much easier, of course), you can only do this if you establish the fact that you are doing a 'dramatised reading' rather than a 'dramatic performance' by standing still. If you can provide reading desks or separate lamps to read by, so much the better. I think it works best if you use any space available by placing the reading stands apart from one another, so that there's some movement present as the listeners have to look from one to the other as each reader takes over. If you don't want to do this, I'm afraid there's no alternative to sitting and learning the lines. Extemporisation with an audience present is very difficult unless you are used to it. So prepare to spend time getting word perfect.

d) If you decide to perform your own group drama, now's the time to start working out whereabouts in the service you would like it to happen. I can immediately think of three places in an overall act of worship where it could be located, the first two drawing attention to the drama itself and its message, the other using it to help people concentrate on the most important part of the service which will take place later on. First, it can be placed squarely in the middle of things, with prayers, hymns, perhaps a suitable reading before it begins and a balancing act of worship afterwards. In this case, what happens before and after relate directly to the central drama. On no account should they be allowed to swamp it. Second, a short service complete in itself may precede the drama, care being taken that the two balance each other properly. (It doesn't seem to work so well the other way round, perhaps because the kind of involvement required for drama can make 'ordinary' worship seem less exciting!) Third, a short drama, not more than five or ten minutes long may be included in the first part of a service centred round a symbolic action, such as a baptism or eucharist. (I can't see any reason why drama shouldn't be included in this supportive role in marriages and funerals too, although I personally have never seen this done.) In this case the drama must tailor itself to the occasion and not distort the service by claiming too much of the limelight. Whichever you decide, make sure that the congregation and its leaders are willing to back whatever it is you have decided to do, and are clear about when you intend to do it.

e) Finally, don't be too proud to ask for help, either in choosing a play or putting it on. Professional help can be obtained from the Religious Drama Association (RADIUS), which exists to encourage drama in worship and drama as worship. Details are given in Appendix I of this book. Some Church of England dioceses have Drama Advisers; otherwise see which local churches can give you a hand.

All these things have to be considered before you actually begin to work together as a group to create what will be your own authentic drama; and they have to be looked at one by one, or at least one of them may well be overlooked. The actual subject you choose is really up to you to decide. I shall be making some suggestions about this in the next section. When you have your material in the shape you want it to be and have cast the people who are going to be in your drama in the roles they are going to play, then you're ready to start rehearsing (and rehearsing and rehearsing ...)

However, whether it's a rehearsal or an actual performance, you can't simply jump into it without any kind of preparation. To rehearse or perform properly, everyone needs to spend a few moments simply warming themselves and each other up. When you warm up you do two things which seem at first contradictory - you become more relaxed and, at the same time, more responsive. You can do this because lessening your bodily tensions allows you to behave in a more spontaneous way, so that you start the play or the rehearsal feeling more fully aware of yourself and your surroundings, more in contact with other people and the play. After all, your aim is to make something come alive. In order to do this you have to feel alive yourself.

C Warming up

There are many things you can do to warm up. Here are some examples. They are suggestions rather than directions. You can adapt them as you wish or find substitutes which you think would be more suitable for your own circumstances.

a) Try imagining you are in a new place, meeting new people. First, explore the room where you are. If it's the place you usually rehearse in, have a look at it as if you've never seen it before. Spread out in the space provided and squeeze into the corners; test the floor out by trying different ways of walking, running, sliding, sitting, lying down. Discover something you've never noticed before. Don't take much notice of anyone else.

b) Gradually begin to be aware of the others. You can do this one person at a time. Find out how many ways you can say hello to people you meet - and try to meet them properly, letting yourself be surprised to see them. Already you're acting! Greet people in different moods - warmly, crossly, resentfully, compassionately, suspiciously, timidly; with pride, humility, forgiveness; as extroverts and introverts; as if you think they know something you don't or you know something *they* don't etc.

c) End up in a circle, enjoying things together. Feel the heaviness of your feet on the floor and the sense this gives you of being in touch with the earth beneath you; stretch up with both arms as if you are reaching for the sun, and embrace its warmth and vigour; taking it into yourself; feel the heavy rain on your head, forehead, face, shoulders, letting your body receive its weight. Then, gradually let it grow lighter, more refreshing, a gentle shower giving way to the sun; share the sunbeams, reflecting them on to other people and receiving them back.

d) An imaginary insect jumps onto your toe, knee, tummy, shoulders, chin, nose, forehead, the top of your head. Each time it alights on you, flick it away so that you move each part of your body in turn. Now it has gone, so you relax each part you tensed to flick it away. (Make sure the backs of your knees are relaxed and also the back of your neck. These are points of tension which affect your whole body.

e) Begin to walk round the room, concentrating all your attention on the parts of your body you've been working with, as if your personality was somehow located in a particular part or organ - your feet, knees, hips; heart, chest, shoulders; mouth, nose, forehead. You'll find that each part you treat in this way will make you feel as though you're a different kind of person. For instance, if you 'lead with your heart' you'll feel concerned, involved, warm towards others; if you concentrate yourself in your forehead then you'll feel intellectual and mentally acute; your nose will simply make you nosier. If you concentrate on your bottom you'll begin to walk in a heavy, lazy way and if your personality shifts to the balls of your feet you'll probably start to walk in a sprightly, alert fashion. This is a fascinating game, creating a sense of being embodied, really present in everything that's going on. It can also help you get to understand the way in which a particular character in a play walks, talks and even thinks and feels, because our personalities are part of *ourselves,* not just something *added on* - and it doesn't matter how well and intelligently you say the lines, you'll never play a part properly if you move, sit or stand in ways that don't fit.

f) You might finish warming up by playing a 'trust game' in order to develop the awareness of working together and depending on one another. Here are two games:

    (i) 'Trust Circle'. The group stands in a circle, arms round one another's shoulders and sways gently first in one direction, then the other. Members volunteer to stand in the middle of the circle and to let themselves relax backwards so that their weight is borne by the circle, one or two of its members catching the volunteer in their arms to prevent them losing their balance and falling. (This isn't as hair-raising as it sounds. I've been doing it for years and I've never known anybody be let drop yet!)

    (ii) 'Blind Walk'. You split up into pairs, one person blindfolding his or her partner and leading them around all the available space. The leader encourages the blindfolded person to touch surfaces and handle objects and then guess what these things are. The walk goes on for about ten minutes, then the blindfold is taken away and leader and follower exchange roles. Strangely enough, people usually begin to enjoy being led in this way. The feel of dependency is reassuring.

g) You can finish by playing a game to 'let off steam'. An example would be 'river bank'. A line is drawn across the middle of the room and the players stand side by side facing it. One player stands apart in order to give the orders. These are quite simple, being either 'On the bank' or 'In the river'. If the first is said, everyone stays exactly where they are; if the second command is given, they jump over the line. The caller varies his/her commands in order to see how many people will get them wrong and end up on the bank when they should be in the river and vice versa. The game goes on until only one person is left in the right place.

All this, of course, takes place beforehand. Afterwards, when the rehearsal or drama itself is over, you may find you want to have an 'unwinding' session when you can share ideas, feelings and impressions of how things have gone. This doesn't need to be a long session and could take place in the relaxed atmosphere of a shared meal or simply a few minutes of discussion and friendly conversation. This always helps people feel a sense of belonging together as a drama group. Recalling what you've been through gives the event *shape*. It is something to which you yourself have contributed in a personal way, and in which your own experience is validated by the others who have taken part with you. (The same effect isn't produced by having a discussion with the audience because this becomes an extension of the drama itself and doesn't allow you to relax at all.)

CHAPTER V: THEMES AND OCCASIONS
Ideas for drama in church

Each of these centres round a particular theme related to Christian worship. I have made some suggestions about ways in which the themes might be expressed and developed in drama. Remember, there are three basic approaches: speech and movement, movement alone, speech alone. Movement may be naturalistic (like ordinary movement, that is) or stylised. Speech may be spoken or read (in various styles). Drama - well that's up to you.

A Creation (Genesis I)

Here the drama is about the problem of making something out of nothing and the amazing way it is solved. This is God's original problem, the greatest one of all. To portray it in a play takes a lot of restraint in order not to try to do too much and end up not doing enough - not enough to avoid looking ridiculous. You may feel, as I do, that the first Genesis account is too important, too significant to be acted in an ordinary, matter of fact, naturalistic way. So you will use symbols to express what is already extremely dramatic. You don't have to dramatise. What you must try and do is use drama to illustrate drama.

In a way this creation drama in the Bible sets the scene for drama everywhere. In it a space is made for something new to take place in, something totally important yet quite simple. Out of darkness a lighted space appears. The effect is to seize our attention. Now we have a world: simply by being light and not darkness we make a world of it. This is not only space but time; it is space waiting to be filled with life. The words of the Bible are mirrored in what is happening, in our own drama of darkness and light.

It's your play, however, and you must decide how this space is to be filled; or even *if* it is to be filled at all. One approach would be to keep all the actors in darkness, placing them at various points around the outer perimeter of the audience and acting area so that their voices come from different parts of the surrounding darkness. This involves dividing them up and getting each person to read a section of the Genesis creation story which they will have to learn by heart, as the glow of torches would certainly ruin the effect. As the narrative proceeds, the lighted circle grows steadily brighter; its ability to focus the audience's attention increases, bringing their own creativity into play and allowing them to give themselves wholeheartedly to the story being told.

Other ways of allowing the story to be seen as well as heard would involve dramatic movement and dance. These approaches are harder to do, however, and really need a lot of skill. Unless you are very talented dancers I wouldn't recommend trying to improve the text in this way. On the other hand, the story is so dramatic it can produce a magnificent effect simply by dividing it up and reading it aloud, particularly if this is done by creating the kind of group sculpture which grows as different orders of creation add themselves to it.

The second Genesis account (Genesis 2) is easier to dramatise because it involves definite characters - Adam, Eve, God, the Serpent. Here again, the area you act in adds to the meaning of the story. One of the characters is definitely the place the story takes place in, the Garden of Eden. You can use lighting to mark out this special location, the first place in the world. If you can't get hold of a spotlight or two (you really need four, one to shine from each point of the compass), try to work out another way of making Eden stand out against its background. I suggest a large round carpet or floor cloth of some kind. The actual biblical dialogue may be preserved intact or perhaps extended into a script, or the whole thing done in mime.

B Journeying Through Life: Pilgrimage

The obvious way to approach this theme would be to illustrate stages in an individual's (or perhaps a church's) progress from birth to death. This could be done with or without words. If no words were used the meaning would be apparent by the use of movement, in this case an obvious progression from one part of the church to another. Perhaps gifts could be exchanged and burdens undertaken or laid aside at significant points on the journey. Certainly there would be barriers to overcome: rivers, mountains, swamps, forests, tunnels etc. There could be a narrator or two to draw attention to particular 'staging posts' and turning points on the journey.

On one level this could be a kind of Pilgrim's Progress drama, inviting the audience to identify with the hero in her or his journey through life. Played with sincerity, the person's difficulties and hardships would create a response in people's hearts and minds and they would feel called on to agree or disagree with the decisions made and the action taken at crucial junctures in the light of their own personal histories. At another level of audience involvement the solutions to human problems offered by the play can be discussed by the audience and compared with its own experiences. Have important things been overlooked, so that the play's balance is changed, affecting its message in some way? Are the conclusions reached acceptable? What parts of the story are the really important staging posts for the hero? Are they the ones to which the drama draws attention or are they different in some way? If there were time, the drama could be re-played in its new revised form. Instead of concentrating on the life of an individual, this kind of drama might trace the life of the congregation itself, thus helping a congregation to arrive at a vision of its own shared history with a view to facing the future together in a spirit of renewal. Drama can be a way of taking part in history, both individual and corporate.

C Work and Wages

Jesus' parables provide marvellous dramas about people involved in carrying out their daily work under various circumstances. For example, 'The Labourers in the Vineyard' (Matt. 20: 1-16), 'The Wicked Husbandmen' (Mark 12: 1-11, Matt. 21: 33-41, Luke 20: 1-18), 'The Doorkeeper' (Mark 13: 34-37, Luke 12: 35-38), 'The Servants Entrusted with Authority' (Matt. 24: 45-51, Luke 12: 42-46), 'The Unjust Steward' (Luke 16: 1-8), 'The Lost Sheep' (Luke 15: 4-7, Matt. 18: 12-14), 'The Sower' (Mark 4: 3-8, Matt. 13: 3-8, Luke 8: 5-8), 'The Tares Among the Wheat' (Matt. 13: 24-30), 'The Patient Husbandman' (Mark 4: 26-29, also Matt. 13: 31-32). The simplest and most direct way of presenting this is as mime, with a commentary, either read from the gospel itself or specially written to relate to the circumstances of a particular performance. An alternative to mime is dance, if you have the confidence and the talent to try this.

Since work (or the absence of it) is such a large part of our daily lives, it provides us with many potential scenarios for church drama. This is an area of life involving a lot of shared experiences, providing settings and situations which will be immediately recognisable to a great many people. In this sense, of course, school is definitely a part of work. If you spend some time thinking of the things that happened to you in school or work, then choose a kind of situation you would like to work on, you shouldn't have any difficulty in making a play out of this. Everybody in the group can contribute something, either as a writer or an actor or both. Everybody's memories are useful, if not in supplying the plot then in adding the details and atmosphere which will make it real for the audience, something they can recognise and enjoy. If actually writing your own play seems beyond the resources available, you might use one of the plots provided by Jesus and produce your own contemporary version. If you have some available musicians you could set the story to music.

Before going to this trouble, however, do make sure that you don't make your production too ambitious for the place provided for it in the service. To do this you may have to check up on two things: the time available and the expectations of the congregation. Remember, people who are used to drama in church react very differently from those who aren't. I have known members of congregations leave the building when faced with a change in the service that they didn't expect. Somehow you have to help people into a frame of mind in which they 'expect the unexpected' and this takes time and patience on the part of everybody concerned. This, certainly, is hard work.

One way to disarm potential opposition is, of course, to involve as many sections of, and age groups in, the congregation as possible in what you're setting out to do. Speak to a lot of people and try to share your own enthusiasm with them; it doesn't take much to get people to feel involved if you speak personally to them and are careful not to ask them to do too much. Remember, it's their support and encouragement you want so tell them this! After all, encouragement is easier to contribute than hard work, and in this case it may turn out to be just as valuable. The time when you do want them to work will come later.

Once the performance has begun and people are sitting in the audience, you can afford to be less tactful. This is the place where you want them to work - and work hard - at enjoying the play and getting everything out of it that there is to get. Here the cliché is more true than ever - the more they put into it the more they will get out of it. In a drama which is actually about work, you could make the point clear, addressing the audience directly and encouraging them to reply, to contribute memories of their own on the subject, so that people really feel part of what is going on. This is the kind of drama which turns into a debate, with everyone working very hard indeed ...

D Here Am I, Send Me

Isaiah, Florence Nightingale, John Wesley, Helen Keller, Gladys Aylward - there are many stories which you could use as a basis for drama on the theme of God's call to men, women and children over the ages. For Christians, of course, everything involving a messenger sent by God and somebody to whom they have been sent always suggests Gabriel and Mary; and if you were simply to mime this kind of meeting you would immediately have your audience thinking about Christmas! At the right season of the year, of course, this would be ideal; but if you were trying to be less specific - for instance, you wanted to express the experience of being called by God as this happens nowadays, to people like us - this extremely powerful image of Christmas might be confusing. I say *might;* I suppose there's no reason why it should, if you're prepared to follow the thought through, but this kind of drama depends on its immediate impression which has to be direct and unambiguous. At the time of year you are doing your play you may not want to be tied in with Christmas in so direct a way.

The obvious way round this, of course, is to seize the nettle and do a play about the Annunciation itself! Again, you have a choice of four ways of approaching this. If you have dancers - and you only need two for this story - this is one of the most immediately suitable incidents in the New Testament to be danced into life; otherwise it can be mimed with the help of a narrator, acted using the biblical dialogue or acted in a modern version in modern idiom. Because the actual story of Mary and Gabriel is short, a different kind of narration might be tried out. You could experiment with the idea of framing the actual Annunciation in a drama involving two (or more) narrators who would provide a contemporary setting for the timeless event - a kind of play within a play. The same kind of thing can, of course, be done with the stories of other people, some well-known, some unknown, who have received a special call from God. The idea of being called in itself, however, really needs a non-specific approach, as in dance or rhythmic movement.

E Revelation and Discovery

Of all themes, this one goes easiest into drama. Drama itself is a kind of revelation - it is the revealing element that makes it dramatic. Even if you are familiar with the story the people in the story itself are not. They are perpetually surprised by what happens. This is straightforward enough, because stories are about unexpected things happening to people, and if there's no surprise there isn't any story - a record, an account, a history, but not a story. What is strange, however, is that audiences and actors are so often taken by surprise by what happens along with the play's characters. Although we know the story, when we become involved in a performance of it we are surprised again (and again and again), because we want things to be revealed to us as to them; we are eager to play their game and pretend we didn't know. We want to know what happens next. The thing to remember is that stages and acting areas always draw attention to themselves simply by being themselves. They are always places of revelation and discovery. It doesn't just depend on the lighting. They are there to show us, and we want to be shown whatever there is to see. Whatever it may be, there is sure to be part of us which will be surprised. This is something you can always depend on. On the stage things don't have to move about in order to surprise us: simply to stand still is to be revealed! This is why revelation and disclosure can be represented statically as effectively as in actual plays. Nowadays we call these dramatic arrangements of motionless figures 'sculpts', and imagine that they are a new invention. Far from it, this way of presenting dramatic encounters and moments of revelation and discovery has been used by Christian congregations for generations. They used to be called 'living pictures' or 'tableaux'. They are the counterpart of the stained glass windows which transform ordinary sunlight into statements of a living faith in so many churches and cathedrals.

As we saw earlier on, there is a difference between tableaux and sculpts, however: sculpts are allowed to move and this can increase their power to communicate. It will only do so, however, so long as it is not abused or overdone. The advantage of sculpts is not to overcome or underplay stillness, but actually to demonstrate it. The movement here is from one stillness to another. It is movement to express contrast. The way that revelation is expressed is by the difference between before and after. It is a way of being quietly dramatic. The accent is on restraint, which can be very moving in the context of the dramatic events portrayed.

Drama itself requires a spontaneous living reaction, in this case confined to the beholder. You may prefer to go for something more along the lines of an actual play in which the moment of revelation itself can be imagined by the audience as they identify with the people in the story and catch something of their amazement, wonder, terror, relief, joy, from the actors trying to relive the event as it actually happened. To try and recapture the emotions of other people is the perennial task of actors. Acting moments of revelation, when the whole world suddenly turns upside down, needs a particular kind of skill. Here, more than anywhere else, you have to learn to let the audience do most of the emotional work. You are acting the part of someone who has been taken by surprise - something that cannot be happening is actually happening. You don't know what to do, how to react ...

You don't know how to react. At the end of the night watch on the battlements at Elsinore, Hamlet is confronted by the ghost of his murdered father. When Richard Burton reached this point in rehearsal, he turned outwards to face the auditorium and said to the director, "What shall I do?" Peter Brook, who was sitting in the stalls, replied, "Do *that,* Richard." Some weeks later, after the play had opened, I was sitting in the audience when this point in Act I was reached. I didn't know what to do, either; neither did anyone else in the audience. I have never forgotten what it felt like though. Nor, I imagine, have they.

F Growth Into The Kingdom

Anything which is about process makes good drama, as all drama is about change. A play is a way of saying 'This is how it was to begin with and how it *later became.*' This doesn't mean you can always see the changes taking place, however. The main point about some plays is that *nothing* changes; but these are also plays about change because the characters and the audience are expecting change to take place and it doesn't appear to be doing so. Actually, there are a lot of plays like this: *The Cherry Orchard* for instance, or *Waiting for Godot.* These are plays which say, 'When is it going to happen?' They aren't usually very dramatic because this isn't a dramatic thing to say; on the other hand, because nothing happens and we feel it should do they make us very conscious of the need for change, the importance of some kind of positive movement in human life. These are dramatic because they frustrate us so much.

There always has to be something frustrating in drama, however. A play in which everything is plain sailing from the beginning through to the end wouldn't really be a play at all. It would certainly be exceedingly boring; and apart from that it would be totally unreal, completely unlifelike. The changes that drama deals with are the issues involved in solving human problems - change brought about by the need to come to grips with the burdens and temptations of being human. Not all human problems are tragic, of course - comedy and farce are about finding solutions to the predicaments we get into in the business of trying to live together. They are about frustration, too, in a way, because they concern the amount of time and effort human beings put into solving problems which are relatively trivial. (As Shakespeare says, *Much Ado About Nothing!*)

The drama we want to present here is anything but trivial. It concerns nothing less than the victory of God's Kingdom over death and sin as this is expressed in the transformation of human ways of living together. It has an epic quality. Any sculpts must be the kind that move (in both senses of the word!). As with 'Pilgrimage', you need to suggest time passing without actually taking too long about it. The difference here, however, is the sheer scope of your subject. You may want to use music and dancing, or perhaps choral speaking, to suggest the passage of long periods of time and the lives and deaths of civilisations. Don't forget, however, that audiences respond more readily to suggestion than direct statement. It's much better to stay simple and succeed than to take on too much and fall flat on your face. Disastrous experiments with artificial smoke and untrustworthy scaffolding have convinced me - and many other people - that an approach which relies on the audience's imagination is by far the best. The more ambitious your theme the fewer things you really need to express it, because of the tendency for all your stuff to get in the way of what the audience have brought with them and are going to get down to using - their own imaginations. Preparing to demonstrate the mighty battle of Agincourt by means of "a few beggarly foils", Shakespeare invites the audience to: "on your imaginary forces work ... into a thousand parts divide one man." You can copy Shakespeare's approach by having a narrator whose job it is to fulfil the task of the Chorus and urge the audience to take part in this positive way, by helping the actors perform the seemingly impossible task of presenting a mighty theme in a kind of theatrical shorthand: "Piece out our imagination with your thoughts."

It's impossible, but it works. So long as it is done with sincerity and conviction, the theme comes alive as soon as it is acted out. Sometimes it's a case of the mightier the story, the fewer actors you need, because a mighty story grips the imagination and spurs the audience to overcome the obvious difficulty involved in the fact that what is happening isn't really at all like the thing it's supposed to represent. Once you really get it going, the human imagination thrives on difficulties like this: the more difficult the better. But you have to get it going. In drama terms, this means that you yourself have to act with sincerity and conviction, really believing that however crudely and inadequately set forth the evidence, the conclusion is true and unshakeable. Which is why we say that drama is about experience rather than argument.

The alternative to presenting this kind of 'reduced epic' is to put together a drama about the effect of the coming of the Kingdom on individuals, with scenes taken from the life and death of ordinary people. The challenge offered to the audience in this case would be that of recognising the extraordinary meaning behind ordinary actions. The same principle applies: the more typical people and events are, the more they are able to point beyond themselves to something unforgettable. As Francis Thompson says, "Move but a stone and start a wing." In this case, perhaps, you wouldn't use any kind of narrator, simply announcing to the audience that what they were going to see was "A short play about the coming of the Kingdom." Let them work out the rest for themselves!

G Faith and Doubt

There's a lot about faith in the Bible. From a drama point of view what concerns us most is that there's a lot about actual people who themselves had faith, whose lives were founded upon and guided by it. There is a list of people like this in Hebrews, chapter 11; any one of these could be the subject of and main character in a drama of faith which could be silently performed with a biblical narration or scripted as an actual play, perhaps including some dialogue taken from the Bible. The simplest approach might be to build up a sculpt out of the people mentioned in the passage using an edited version of Hebrews as a commentary. One by one the people mentioned would join the group to create a living image of faith.

The healing stories of Jesus provide even better material, as does the account of Jesus and Peter walking on the sea (Matt 14: 22-32). Jesus tells many people that it is in fact their own faith which has healed them. We aren't given much background to many of these stories (The Man Born Blind is an exception, as is the Raising of Lazarus.), consequently there are some good opportunities for illustrating the idea of faith by writing a short play about someone in the Bible who had it.

They don't need to be in the Bible, however. The essence of faith is how it presents itself, not where we read about it. It seems to me that the most characteristic thing about it is its solitary nature. He or she who stands by faith alone, very often *has* to stand alone. As we pointed out before, a single figure on a stage commands more attention than a group, certainly more than a crowd of people.

Then, of course, there's the other side of things. It's always the presence of doubt that makes us aware of faith. So we're dealing here with a double subject, something which directly implies the opposite. The lonely figure on the stage is sustained by faith, but besieged by uncertainties, undermined by fears. Drama is built into human faith, as individuals and communities struggle towards 'the hope that they have grasped'. Not only single figures, but groups of people can represent this on the stage, or within the space set apart for drama. I think it is very important when illustrating the triumph of faith over doubt, whether it be in groups or individuals, nations of families, to show the cost as well. The simple fact is that if you don't bring home your own appreciation (experience?) of how difficult it can be to have faith, and how some of the things that happen can make it even more difficult, you run the risk of alienating at least some of your audience, who are likely to go away muttering to themselves, "Easy for some!"

H Justice and Mercy

Another two things that go closely together. At least they do if we mean the justice and mercy of God. God's mercy is the opposite of his justice; his justice makes demands upon us that we cannot fulfil and his mercy fulfils them on our behalf. His mercy is, for us, another way of talking about his love. This has to be pointed out because a lot of people mean 'being fair' when they talk about justice, and the opposite of this is 'being unfair' which, in many cases, isn't being merciful at all! Christian dramas about justice and mercy try to present our response about God's demands of love; in other words, in one way or another they show us Jesus. The greatest Christian drama is the Eucharist. It is also the ultimate presentation of justice and mercy. Justice and mercy are opposites in the sense that the second satisfies the first but doesn't in any way negate it.

You'll find that Christian dramas on subject of mercy and justice will turn out to be celebrations of God's love. They will be about timeless and placeless things, events taking place in Eternity. Because you're dealing with a subject that is beyond the reaches of our human ability to work things out, your drama will be symbolic rather than literal - by which I mean that the people in it will represent more than they are. They are ordinary human beings but what they act out will stand for the action of God. At least, that's our intention.

This doesn't necessarily mean that you're limited to movement-plus-narration or group sculpts, however. The difference between human ideas about justice and mercy and the mercy and justice of God has always been a particularly rich source on inspiration for playwrights (for example, Arthur Miller's *The Crucible*). This is a difficult theme to pursue, not because it is not dramatic - it's certainly that - but because our own ideas about what is and isn't 'fair', on the one hand, and the human tendency to find some kinds of behaviour unforgivable on the other, tend to get in the way. The kind of forgiveness God shows us in Jesus is particularly hard to take in. This isn't because we ourselves can't forgive some things, but because we're not at all sure they ought to be forgiven. A drama which contrasted God's forgiveness and love with our own drastically limited movements in that direction would certainly have an impact. You could, for instance, use Bertolt Brecht's approach and do the same drama twice over: the first time allowing the outcome to depend on human ideas of justice and 'fairness', the second time allowing it to reflect the love and mercy of God himself.

I Forgiveness and Acceptance

The Bible is a book about God's forgiveness. There are many stories in it about the way his forgiveness has given new life to men and women who have called on his Name. As the psalms make abundantly clear, the Jews saw, and see, their history as a succession of occasions of repentance and forgiveness, experiences of falling by the wayside and then being re-established on their long journey to the Kingdom (see particularly Pss 105-107). All this involved entire nations, yet it can be portrayed with a few actors who are willing to invite and use the imagination of the audience. It can also be danced or sung, or described by narrators arranged at different points in and around the acting area. Lighting could be used to illuminate strategic points in the journey through history.

One story in the New Testament stands out as the final statement on forgiveness. The parable of the Prodigal Son is a powerful drama of forgiveness and acceptance; more than this, it is Jesus' own choice of story, his chosen way to express the nature of God in terms that human beings can understand. In a sense, to choose to present forgiveness in terms of another drama, another story, seems to be perverse, ungrateful even. Having said that, however, other stories can be told which relate to this one like variations on a musical theme. This story is so well known and so fundamental to people's experience of God in their own lives, that any drama which has a similar plot will have an impact. Whether the original will be more powerful because it *is* the original, the story as Jesus told it, or a contemporary 'realisation' might, in particular circumstances, strike nearer home, you as a group must decide for yourselves.

Part of the power of the story lies in its shape; it has a very clear beginning, middle and end, and the central section telling of the younger son's adventures and trials is a very striking example of the chaos which lies at the heart of all stories about real changes in human lives, just as the restoration which constitutes the final stage is the most wonderful consummation. Stories with this shape, as we have seen, will always 'pack a punch' because they are about the most important things in life, things which will always involve an onward movement towards a better way of being. This story's shape and theme coincide: it is about growth of relationship and the love which overcomes obstacles that get in its way. As a drama it cannot fail to make its mark. This story really is about life and death, as Christians see it - that is, living, dying and rising to new life.

J Pride and Humility

The story of the Publican and the Sinner (Luke 18, 10-44) provides a marvellous opportunity for a very simple but also very effective piece of drama. Humility and pride are personal characteristics or attitudes of mind and soul which not only affect the way that people behave but do so in a way which is immediately obvious to other people from their actual bodily attitudes - the way that they stand and sit, walk about, make gestures. Everything a proud or humble individual does with her or his body can be a way of revealing pride or humility. The two states of mind are dramatically presented by themselves, and even more dramatically opposed to each other.

Here again, however, as with justice and mercy, there is a real difference between the way in which people usually talk about these things and the way that the Bible regards them. Pride is often regarded as a virtue and humility as a sense of shame, either because we *feel* humble (we 'don't stand up for ourselves') or actually *are* humble (we are too far down the social scale). Often these two reasons relate directly to each other. The Bible, however, tells us we should love God and our neighbours as ourselves. For the Bible, therefore, humility means being aware of our failure to do these two things; pride means thinking we actually *do* do them. The pride portrayed in Jesus' story isn't the same thing at all as the respect and regard we should have for ourselves as creatures of God made in his image - which, Jesus says, should equal the very respect and regard we should have for our fellow men and women, who are also God's children. The pride shown by the Publican is sheer vainglorious self-celebration, as he congratulates himself for being 'well in' with God.

Just how different is this from the things we are proud about? How is it that the Sinner's humility justifies him while in our own world humility and inferiority, self-knowledge and depression are so often confused? This difference certainly lends itself to being explored in drama: two kinds of humility, two kinds of pride. This could be done by presenting the biblical scene, either with the original dialogue spoken by the actors performing it or silently with a biblical narration; it could be sculpted, using both group and individual sculpts; it could be the basis for expressive use of movement and/or dance; lighting could be used to mark and separate realms of pride and humility, actual physical locations within the acting area. On the other hand, a new drama could be put together dealing with the same theme in circumstances which either correspond to the original ones or are contrasted with them (or both!). Finally, the original drama could be extended into a scenario involving an actual meeting of the two men and their ensuing relationship.

In all these approaches, somebody who believes themselves to be in charge of, or superior to others is shown in contrast to somebody who assumes the opposite role. If these two are brought into personal contact, you have one of the most dramatically effective of all theatrical conventions - the story of 'the worm that turned'.

K Self-Discovery and Sharing

I've put these two things together because what I have in mind here is the kind of sharing which concerns more than shared ideas or even shared feelings although both these things are very important. What I want to look at here is *sharing the self* with someone else. This is what they used to call 'baring the soul'. Nowadays, however, we talk about 'self-disclosure'. It means really being honest with ourselves about ourselves and letting someone else in on what we find.

As we said earlier, plays can have a lot to do with this sort of thing. You might think they would get in the way, because a play is something you or someone else has made up, and what we're looking for here is one person showing another what they are really like. A play is a medium of communication and as such it comes between two sets of people, those who put it together and then put it on, and those who make up the audience. So far as direct contact is concerned, a play stands in the way.

But it doesn't *get* in the way. Just the opposite. Plays are doors not barriers. They let the people out of one place into another. Sometimes we need drama in order to release us from our confinement. It's as if we are shut up in our ideas and attitudes, our opinions and feelings, as if we were each one of us locked up in a room kept clear of any furniture except our own. A play which involves us in a world which is like ours - a world of people who suffer and rejoice just like us and even, when it comes to the most important things in life, actually think like us - and yet is not ours. Not ours to keep locked away from others. Plays are places for open doors and shared experiences, shared *discoveries.* In them our worlds are widened and we reach out towards others.

I can think of several good reasons why we're so good at keeping our thoughts and feelings hidden in this way. The most obvious one is cultural - we admire the stiff upper lip which refuses to let feelings through, particularly if they are feelings of distress about oneself. Other reasons are more personal. First, these feelings could be painful to think about; if we admit to having them we remind ourselves of what we would rather forget. Second, we reveal things about ourselves to other people and lay ourselves wide open, we think, to the chance of being rejected by them. If we don't show our real selves to anyone else, whoever is angry, contemptuous or rejecting towards us won't be able to reach the real us at all, so to that extent we feel we're safe. Third, we don't want to impose them on others. In other words, our reasons for avoiding self-disclosure are to do with social rules we have been taught, defensiveness we have developed and shyness we instinctively feel in the presence of people we don't know very well.

As I suggested earlier on, a play is a kind of game we agree to play with other people. While we are playing we lay down our arms, by which I mean our *defences,* and allow people to feel what we feel and see things as we see them. How can we do this if, in the play, we are playing the part of someone whose feelings we don't share and whose opinions we definitely disagree with? How can this be a way of letting our true selves be seen?

To be willing to be in a play at all and 'perform' in front of other people is a way of focusing attention on yourself. You wouldn't do this unless you had some kind of protection. Celebrities have a 'public personality': actors, a part supplied by someone else. All the same, as anyone who has stood trembling in the wings knows, it takes a good deal of courage to go on stage, even in character. You are terrifyingly conscious of 'putting yourself on the line' in a way nobody else ever asks you to do. When it comes down to it, going on stage like this you feel that it isn't your opinions and attitudes, even your motives and feelings that are being exposed and potentially judged, but *you* - your actual *self*. This is true whatever part you may have undertaken to play in the drama. If acting is a way of using stage characters in order to let our real selves be seen, it allows you to use parts of yourself which you would prefer to keep hidden - and *particularly* if you are playing someone you don't admire at all. Why is it you don't admire them? Is it because they say and do and feel things you wouldn't dream of doing? Perhaps you should remember some of your own fantasies; even your actual *dreams* ... Acting provides us with a way of coming clean about ourselves. Being in plays is an opportunity to reach out and say how much we both need one another and are, given a lot of help, willing to entrust ourselves to one another. Acting gives us a bit of help.

This is a fundamental fact about all kinds of drama, whether it is spoken, sung, mimed, danced or sculpted. Drama is a way of acknowledging the sort of truth about ourselves which cries out louder the more we try to silence it. To let other people in on this kind of secret is the only way we can ease its burden. Left to ourselves we try all kinds of ways of pretending that it isn't real; and that one way or another, we are making it up. The fact is that we shall never be able to do anything about our deception unless we have the courage to acknowledge its real existence: to do this properly we need other people to share our secret with, so that it can come out into the open as part of our shared reality. To be healed and forgiven we must be willing to show ourselves as we feel we really are. We must be *both challenged and loved.*

In two places in St John's Gospel we can see this process at work in Jesus' ministry very clearly indeed. In Chapter 3 he receives an unofficial visit from a member of the religious elite who comes to him under the shadow of darkness to reassure himself that there isn't any really urgent need for people to change in any way, himself included, by speaking to a teacher come from God. Jesus challenges him with the greatest change and the brightest light of all - See what you need! See *yourself*... We know from the last part of the Gospel that Nicodemus's life was changed by his meeting with Jesus. In Chapter 4 Jesus talks to the Samaritan woman whom he has met at Jacob's Well. She too has things on her mind which she has difficulty dealing with or forgetting. What he says to her sends her rushing away to share her healing with others: "Come and see a man who told me everything I ever did" (v29). The account of Jesus' two followers on their journey to Emmaeus leads up to a moment of disclosure on Jesus' part which reaches to the heart of their grief. On the road he listened and talked, encouraging them to open up their hearts and reveal the depths of their suffering; now here in the inn he is "recognised by them at the breaking of the bread" (Luke 24:35)

These are powerful dramas. Whichever way you decide to present them they will involve your audience and actors within a deeper experience of the Gospel, a shared encounter with Jesus in which "the secret thoughts of many will be laid bare" (Lk 2:35). This is because they use a means of revelation to embody a message about sharing. With or without a narrator, using modern settings and dialogue or reproducing the originals, creating your own dramas on the same themes or presenting the events exactly as they are described in the Bible, motionless as sculpts or in animated dance sequences, these stories and others like them are dramatic enough to present themselves by themselves.

L Between-ness and Letting-Be

This theme follows more or less directly on from the last one and a lot of what was said there applies here as well. If your theme is human relationship you can't use the kind of drama which doesn't allow your audience any freedom to question what you're saying - or rather, what your play is saying. I have seen many groups make use of drama as an opportunity to lay down the law on a particular subject. If your message is about relationship your methods must be relational; just as if you're talking about love you should show it to your audience; if your play is about friendship, be friendly towards them... Don't forget, they can't answer you back, unless you invite them to do so - and even then they're at a disadvantage, because to be someone in the play is always to be in a dominant position vis-à-vis a member of the audience. Look how the performers bully their audience in a pantomime! If you're in the audience the only way you can assert yourself is by walking out - and even that doesn't cut very much ice unless everybody does it. The relationship between artists and audience should be a gentle one, one of persuasion rather than force, and it is the actor's responsibility to see that it is.

I'm sorry to keep repeating this. I wouldn't do if it wasn't for the fact that I know so very well how easily drama can be used as a kind of emotional blackmail to twist the souls of a congregation. I've often seen it used like this, sometimes by people who really ought to have known better. It's done in the name of evangelism and used specifically for that purpose. Re-assuring as it may be to the converted to hear the Gospel driven home like this it isn't actually an efficient way of making new Christians. In order to do this we have to let the gospel speak for itself. Anything else builds up a resistance. Drama is exactly that - a way of letting the word speak for itself, so that it is free to exert its own power.

The inspired preaching of the first apostles certainly moved the hearts and minds of the men, women and children who heard them; many of the most striking conversions of all however arose out of things that happened to people in the ordinary routines of their daily life. Saul-Paul, in the course of his anti-Christian police-duties; all those who Jesus healed, in market places, on street corners or in country lanes; even Nathaniel under his fig-tree - each of these found, or was found by Jesus in a non-church setting. The ability of drama to present marvellous things in ordinary ways is its greatest advantage for evangelism. Drama shows a congregation where something valuable may be found, something which may, for them, turn out to be the 'pearl of great price'. It hands them a shovel, but doesn't force them to dig. Nor should it do the digging for them. Letting-be can be the actual theme of the drama expressed in stories about people who in bestowing liberty on others, find their own freedom. These can be acted as ordinary straightforward drama, or mimed or moved or danced. As with the other themes discussed here the meaning may be laid open indirectly by presenting a contrasting scenario concerned with what happens when you impose yourself and your version of reality upon other people and expect them to respond in a wholehearted way, with imagination and creativity.

The drama of letting be depends mainly on symbolism - images and ideas that speak for themselves, reaching out to us and using our language to make their meaning clear. Remember, the stage is a magic area, within which things have a strange power to speak for themselves. And what they say, left to themselves, will certainly be more than you expected.

M Balance and Wholeness
This is an area in which words may actually get in the way,

because there are so many ways that balance and wholeness can be realised in a dramatic way using other means of communication. Dance is the obvious choice, of course, and if you have a group of dancers you would be advised to leave most of the work to them. The idea of balance is most vividly expressed in patterns and shapes, and so movement will be essential. On the other hand the kind of movement involved could be quite simple. You don't need a *corps de ballet* to get the idea across; you do need to make sure that you practice moving in ways that are precise, controlled, flexible, and clearly defined. Without being gymnasts those involved are going to have to use their bodies in order to express ideas and feelings instead of depending on words to get their meaning across. In fact, ideas like balance and wholeness can be expressed by a sole performer who knows how to embody them in movement and gesture. Anyone who has seen Roly Bain, the founder-president of the Order of Holy Fools, instructing a congregation as to the difficulties and dangers of "the Christian path", using a slack rope, a parasol and an arm full of wooden rings to do so, will understand what I mean! You don't need to be as skilful as Roly to get the idea across, but you will have to concentrate very hard, and not blur the outline of the moving picture you create.

Except of course to provide contrast. What you do won't express balance and perfection by itself unless you manage to do it very skilfully indeed. You can get away with being a good deal less skilful if you make your point about the difficulty of attaining perfection by providing striking evidence of the opposite. There's nothing like a conspicuous failure for bringing home the difficulties involved in achieving success. Even Roly has to fall off sometimes to stop it looking too easy. If your balanced moment grows out of some kind of chaos, you'll make your point much clearer. (Having said that, however, it should be noted that in drama even chaos has to be 'carefully designed': things that get out of hand have to do so in the right way. This, too, takes rehearsal!)

Balance and wholeness are, of course, properties of the stories Jesus told, as they are of all genuine story-telling. Because this is so, every time you act out one of the parables the way he actually told it, preserving its original shape and not trying to improve it any way by adding extra incidents or omitting parts you may not like so much, something of this balance comes across to the congregation. Perfect truth is embodied in perfect form, an order of events expressing the wholeness of God's purpose.

These are some thoughts about the way in which drama can be used as a part of worship when the actual service is arranged around a particular theme. I've chosen some possible themes as they occurred to me, and this list is obviously inadequate. At the same time I don't think it would be possible to draw up a really satisfactory one, there are so many things you might want to draw attention to in a worship setting. As it stands, there is one big gap in the suggestions I have made; I've left out - or rather refrained from including - a section specifically about Resurrection. I've done this on purpose, however. I think I've done enough; time now to hand things over to you. If there are other themes you'd like to be thinking about and planning for, now's the time to get started. So there you are - over to you. *You* do the Resurrection yourselves!

CHAPTER VI: DRAMA FOR SPECIAL OCCASIONS

Up to now we have been looking at some ways in which drama can contribute as a part of an ordinary weekly service in church: drama to illustrate and enrich some of the themes which occur in our worship. Traditionally speaking drama has been used to mark special events in the Church's year, such as Christmas and Easter, Pentecost, Corpus Christi etc. The idea of celebrating a very special 'day in the life of' has people saying let's do a play, why don't we put a play on? Often it doesn't get much further than that. People tend to have fixed ideas about what is involved, and it all seems too much like hard work... All the same, drama and special occasions do go together, because the remembrance of important things that happened in the past brings with it the urge to relive them in some way, to make these feelings and ideas alive again, to live them again for ourselves...

The same kind of thing happens when it comes to celebrating more personal events, things concerning individuals and groups of people within the wider church. Breaking bread and drinking wine, the fellowship meal of the group of Christians who come together at a particular place and time, to be the church there, is a drama of the last supper where meaning begins with the life death and rising again of Jesus and widens outward to embrace all places and times, all lives. If we follow this up and look at some of the ways we celebrate particular land-marks in people's personal lives we will find that the ceremonies associated with them are dramas too. Baptism and Confirmation, the symbolic washing and laying on of hands, repeat the actions of Christians who performed these gestures in Gospel times as outward signs of spiritual grace: both resonate personal meaning in the way that drama does, by repeating words and gestures associated with an incarnate Lord. In this sense, marriages and funerals do the same, as rings are lovingly exchanged, and earth laid upon earth 'in sure and certain hope'.

These things make drama a natural choice for marking the stages in life's journey, either to celebrate our having got so far or to provide ourselves with a memory for the future, something to look back on and recall how we felt at the time, how life appeared to us then. In practical terms, we need staging posts in order to make sense of our personal chronologies so that things that happen to us can be seen in relation to them; for example, such and such a thing happened 'before Mary's graduation' or 'after the service we had to say goodbye to Pastor Andrews'. These events were more than pegs to hang memories on, so we won't appear to have forgotten when, where and what has been going on during our lives; they also remind us of fundamentally important matters, too. They remind us *why* things were going on, what all this activity meant to the people involved. They are access-points for the truth that does not change or grow old. Ribbons tied round trees. Pledges of love.

Dramas put together to remember things that have happened in the past will work like rites of passage because drama and ritual both recall the past in the same way. We saw how this happens earlier on in this book. Both drama and ritual present events as having a special relationship among them, a relationship of 'before' and 'after' which is full of meaning and symbolises an over-riding purpose in being alive. They may not always spell this out, but their action always asserts that this is in fact the case. It is not an easy or inevitable relationship: between 'before and after' something difficult or even painful has been accomplished. In its purest, most expressive, most dramatic form, it is always a kind of victory. Relationship, meaning, love imply an overcoming.

Drama is a passage to higher ground. Because of this it has the power to affect the circumstances in which it is being performed. A straightforward service of worship and prayer, once it contains drama becomes a rite of passage. The prayers, hymns and songs, readings and sermon, which precede and follow it, all become ways of announcing and finally establishing a meaning which is presented in a living way by the drama at the centre.

The following are some typical occasions for presenting this kind of 'staging post drama':

a) <u>To celebrate the birth of a child.</u>

This would be about welcome, acceptance, arrival, the reception of a new human being by the rest of the human race. It is an initiation into the condition of being alive at all, so it predates Baptism. It would be a celebration of the ways that families are bonded together. It shouldn't, I think, imply commitment to the Christian Church on the part of the parents, but simply be offered as the Church's gift to them in celebration.

<u>Drama</u> might portray the wonder and confusion of the new baby's first vision of the world, and the comfort given by the mother and father.

b) <u>Achieving Adult Membership of the Congregation</u>

In some Christian denominations, full membership of the Church comes with Confirmation. However this may, and often does take place at a comparatively early age, several years before the candidate would be old enough to take a share of the responsibility for the way in which his or her church is actually run. The purpose of this drama would be to establish some kind of landmark in developing personal maturity and willingness to become involved in church life. <u>Drama</u> should centre upon some kind of conflict involved in gaining acceptance as somebody entitled to have a share in deciding how the church should be run.

c) <u>When a Son or Daughter Leaves Home</u>
Another dramatic situation marking the end of childhood and the point at which someone sets out into the adult world. Perhaps somebody is about to fulfil a personal ambition, something they have dreamed about for a long time; perhaps they must say goodbye to family and friends and actually leave the country; perhaps someone is starting their first real job, or their first away from home, or one which represents an important change in the direction of their lives.
<u>Drama:</u> Somebody has to find their own way amid conflicting responsibilities, ambitions, doubts about their ability to survive; they have to find out who they are and what to do with their life. Where does help come from?

d) <u>Marking an Engagement</u>
Of all the undertakings we make in life, agreeing to marry someone is certainly one of the most considerable, involving far-reaching changes in the way we see ourselves and organise our lives. Even when we have decided to embark on this personal revolution, we need time to work through the experience of making such a decision. Because of the assumption of such importance by a single relationship within the whole network of personal relationships, life must be reorganised; and not only the two lives which are most intimately concerned, because marriage is an alliance between families and social groups.
<u>Drama:</u> Personal encounters set against a background of the relationship between different social groups; manoeuvring and negotiations between parties; difficulties help to join two people closer together. (You wouldn't need to go quite so far as Romeo and Juliet!)

e) Welcoming a Family into the Congregation

Some people prefer to creep in unannounced and sit at the back, pretending they've been coming to this church for years. Most of us probably prefer to ease ourselves into belonging rather than attract too much attention to begin with. However, there comes a time when we really want to feel we belong, and would like our fellow worshippers to recognise the fact. Apart from this, new families move into the district and a welcome at church can be one of the things that takes the edge off all the strangeness and newness; and not only new families, but individual men and women, people as yet unbaptised, those looking for somewhere to start going to church for the first time etc etc. All could do with a welcome.

Drama: This could be an opportunity for a dramatised tour of the church, with contributions from various church members either as themselves or 'in role'; or a drama about home-coming.

f) Saying Goodbye to a Family who are Emigrating

This is an undertaking that deserves to be properly celebrated because of the courage and determination required from those taking part. A church service is a way in which you would give shape to thoughts and feelings which are still not properly assimilated by those involved because the size of the project gets in the way. At another level, the idea of travelling overseas suggests changes that are very deep indeed, because water is seen as the natural symbol of profound life changes. Many initiation ceremonies throughout the world make use of water in this way, as well as Baptism.

Drama: Real changes involve the disorganisation of old patterns of life in readiness for new ones to emerge. If you can create images of the sea, with dance, mime or sculpt, you will suggest the idea of a sea-change, calm after storm.

g) Saying Goodbye to a Minister

In the Church of England, services welcoming the clergy are well-established. However, there isn't one for bidding them farewell when they leave the parish. By including drama within an ordinary service you could make it into a rite of passage to mark an important stage in the minister's life - not forgetting the family, too.

Drama: Just as Induction services traditionally involve a ceremonial tour of the church - bells, pulpit, lectern etc - now you could do the same thing the other way round; or you could recapture a typical incident in her or his ministry and present it in a way that would be witty and appreciative. (Drama depends on conflict - but that doesn't mean your touch has to be heavy!)

h) Giving Thanks for Recovery from Illness

The aim here is to combine the idea of getting better oneself with that of being able to take part in things again alongside other people. This doesn't necessarily mean you have been shut away in hospital, but you have been unable for some time to take the active part in the lives of the people around you which is so fundamental to your own sense of identity. You may also be very conscious of the strain your own illness has imposed on others. We don't always behave as well as we'd like to when we're ill or in pain; on the other hand, not everybody will feel they have been as patient with us as they would like to have been. This is an opportunity to say thank you to other people and to God, and to make a new start.

Drama: Something symbolising a breakdown in health (and perhaps some aspects of relationship) and the subsequent feelings of relief, joy and thankfulness. You may want to use words, but this kind of theme is powerfully expressed in physical movement from one 'state of life' to another, via the place of difficulty and pain.

i) Facing Retirement

Retirement can be very critical for some people. As fewer and fewer are needed to carry out a widening range of work tasks, men and women are likely to find themselves having to give up paid work at an increasingly early age. The feeling of being put on the scrap heap when you're still at the height of your powers is likely to grow more widespread. There's a tendency for people to deny this by saying something like "I'm used to holding down a difficult job. I can cope with any emotional difficulties involved in having to retire, thank you very much!" The purpose of drama here would be to bring these matters to light so that they can be acknowledged and, with a bit of help and understanding, lived through.

Drama: A voyage into the unknown, in which familiar landscapes are gradually left behind; support comes from unexpected quarters, and confidence grows as new contacts are made and skills learned ... there could be movement from space to space, with the gradual increase of lighting; objects and sculpts can be used to symbolise occupations and interests.

j) Renewal

Periods of change in the life of a congregation may also be times of genuine renewal, if we have the faith to see them like that! Because we don't always welcome the things that interrupt and change our normal, well-established ways of working and worshipping together, we always need to remind one another of God's steadfast love for us in Christ and the ways in which he reveals that love to us - ways which often seem unlikely, or even downright impossible.

Our experience of God's love is many things: one of these is through these miraculous shifts in life that we wonder at and so quickly forget or take for granted. In 'growing into Christ' spontaneity and patience go hand in hand. Here drama contributes to people's consciousness of change as an opportunity for renewal, and dramatic change as the direct intervention of God into human lives.

Drama: Poetry, music, dance, lighting effects, symbolising the breaking down of barriers between different groups of people present in church, and between the whole congregation and the world outside the walls; movement expressing the reversal of expectation and the formation of new patterns.

EPILOGUE

We have come a long way from Ann's improvised solo drama about the child in the concentration camp. In the last section, for instance, we have been considering drama used to celebrate widespread changes in entire congregations. In fact, most of the things we have been looking at have involved more than a single performer. Many have needed dialogue too, not to mention carefully planned and rehearsed movements and gestures. Sometimes there has been music and special kinds of lighting effects. Whereas Ann did it all by herself.

Nevertheless, the things Ann used are the same ones we have been thinking about using. First of all, she used her imagination to create a particular place and time. Second, she focused her imagination by using a special space - an ordinary space made special by concentrating her own and other people's attention to it. Thirdly, although she didn't ever speak aloud, her face and body spoke for her as she concentrated on communicating with her doll and shut out everything else. Fourth, she showed when the play began and when it ended. Fifth, she used what was happening to the doll, the doll's story, to illustrate her own.

In fact, there was even less difference than this. The most striking thing of all about Ann's performance was the way she managed to make a play out of nothing except imagination and the presence of a few people. She didn't need other people to be members of her cast - but she did need them to be an audience. This was the only other thing required. Herself and her audience were the basic raw materials; out of this she conjured her own theatre and transformed an idea into a performance. For this was no solo: it owed its existence to the people watching almost as much as to Ann herself, as, picking up the message that there might be something worth seeing, we instinctively drew together to form a ring around her, making a space magical enough for a play to take shape in.

APPENDIX
The Religious Drama Society of Great Britain ('Radius')

Radius is a national body, working with all Christian churches, the theatre and voluntary organisations. It exists to encourage drama which illuminates the human condition, It aims to help local Church congregations and creative groups to a deeper understanding of the value of all types of drama, and supplies the background of direction and technical advice to reach proper standards in the presentation of plays. An annual Summer School of Drama is held each August.

The Radius library can be highly recommended. It is open on Tuesdays and Thursdays, from 11.00 a.m. to 3.30 p.m. and members may borrow five single copies of plays and books at a time. Sets of plays for play-reading or production can be hired for a small fee. The Librarians will advise on suitable plays for specified occasions.

The Radius office is at Christ Church and Upton Chapel, 1a Kennington Road, London SE1 7QP. (Tel: 0171 401 2422)

SOME BOOKS

Bain, R.   *Fools Rush In.* London: Harper Collins 1993

Barker, C.   *Theatre Games.* Methuen 1977

Berry, C.   *Your Voice and How to Use It.* Harrap 1975

Brook, P.   *The Empty Space.* MacGibbon & Kee 1968

Burridge, P.   *Time to Act.* Hodder & Stoughton 1979
& Watts, M.

Burridge, P.   *Lightning Sketches.* Hodder & Stoughton 1981
& Watts, M.

Clark, B.   *Group Theatre.* Pitman 1971

Grainger, R.   *Presenting Drama in Church.* Epworth 1986

Grainger, R.   *The Beckoning Bible.* Methodist Publishing House, 2001

Hodgson, J. (ed)   *The Uses of Drama.* Eyre Methuen 1972

Pickering, K.V.   *Drama in the Cathedral.* Churchman 1984

Read, S.   *Christian Theatre: A Handbook for Church Groups.*
& Fry, R.   Eyre & Spottiswood 1986

Scheff, T.J.   *Catharsis in Healing, Ritual and Drama.* University of
California 1979

Slade, P.   *Child Play.* Kingsley 1976

Spolin, V.   *Improvisation for the Theatre.* Pitman 1963

Watts, M.   *Christianity and The Theatre.* Handsel Press 1986